THE QANON FILES
The Essential Guide to the Great Awakening

MR. BABYLON

I. QANON DECODED - THE AWAKENING BEGINS

CONTENTS

I. QANON DECODED - THE AWAKENING BEGINS

Introduction	5
1. WHO IS Q AND WHAT THE HELL IS THE QANON MOVEMENT?	9
Who Is Q?	10
How Did QAnon Start?	12
2. THE MAIN THEORIES OF Q'S IDENTITY, IS TRUMP INVOLVED?	15
The Stirrings of The QAnon Movement	19
3. THE GLOBAL AWAKENING: THE FIGHT AGAINST THE EVIL	21
4. THE DEEP STATE: A SECRET PLAN TO GOVERN THE WORLD	25
Who Has the Knowledge?	28
Disentangling the Message	28
5. THE MOST POPULAR Q'S PREDICTIONS I	30
6. THE MOST POPULAR Q'S PREDICTIONS II	36
7. THE MEDIA AND FAKE NEWS: A WAR HAS BEGAN	42
Trump Defies the Globalists	43
And Then Came Q-Anon!	43
The Pedo-Monster Art of Alex Podesta	47
8. HOW THE PATRIOTS FIGHT THE ENEMY?	48
9. THE OLD DEEP STATE PUPPETS	51
10. THE NEW DEEP STATE PUPPETS	56
Operation Mockingbird	56
Operation Paperclip	59
11. WHAT IS A CONSPIRACY THEORY?	62
A New Phenomenon?	64
What Is A False Flag?	65

12. WHAT IS THE INFORMATION WAR?	68
Why Is the Information War Necessary?	69
Statement of The Pentagon	71
Cultivating Warfare Experts	73
13. WHO MET Q?	74
Tom Lewis	74
14. GLOBAL ELITES OF THE NEW WORLD ORDER	77

II. QANON UNLOCKED - SECRETS FROM THE SOURCE

Introduction	85
1. WHO IS Q? IS TRUMP RELATED? WHERE CAN I READ HIS MESSAGES?	89
2. HOW TO DECIPHER Q'S DROPS?	92
Learning the Lingo of The Chans	97
3. THE TENTACLES OF THE DEEP STATE	98
The Politically Purported Truth	98
Europeans Need to Dispose of The European Union	100
4. THE PEOPLE BEHIND THE DEEP STATE	103
5. THE EPSTEIN CASE AND HIS FAMOUS CONNECTIONS	106
6. THE STORM IS COMING: THE 2020'S DECADE	112
7. DONALD TRUMP - WILD CARD	118
Court Cases and Bankruptcies	120
Run for The White House	120
Hard Times and Dirty Tricks	121
Smear by Smut	122
8. SYMBOLISMS	124
9. MORE ON SYMBOLISM	132
Sacred Geometry	135
10. THE NEW WORLD ORDER TIMETABLE	137
11. IMMIGRATION, WITCH HUNTS AND HEALTH CARE	141

12. HOSTILE MIND TAKEOVER 146
   Only One Conclusion 146
   The Same Phrase 148
   Too Many Questions 150
   When Fear Bends Your Mind 150
   Isolation and Brainwashing 151
   Brainwashing in Advertising 152

13. JOHN F. KENNEDY'S ASSASSINATION 153
   Glossary 157

Conclusion 165

INTRODUCTION

For those of you who have heard of QAnon, but only have a vague idea of what it is really all about, I'll provide a brief overview here.

In short form, QAnon is a conspiracy theory that alleges a vast, worldwide scheme by Evil Doers in the USA and abroad, known collectively as "the Deep State," to do lots of really bad things and keep doing them. There may also be a larger purpose or end game here— establishing the "New World Order" or some such—but it's not very clear. In fact, it seems (not surprisingly, when you look into the specifics) that the advocates for this theory can't quite agree on what the specific agenda of the Evil Doers is, other than to keep being really, really bad.

Fighting against the cabal of Evil Doers is a pair of heroes. The first of these great champions is Q, aka QAnon. Ostensibly a high-ranking member of the Trump administration with a military intelligence background, this nameless, faceless individual provides information—sporadically—via what are known as "drops." These are just coded pieces of text, called "crumbs," which further must be deciphered in order to have any meaning at all. Doing this are self-appointed Q interpreters, known as "bakers," who take the crumbs and cook them into something with meaning. Well, theoretically.

INTRODUCTION

Aiding Q in his selfless fight, tooth and nail against the Deep State, is our second hero: Donald J. Trump. Yep! He of the 10 days of golf per month, and 4-6 hours of TV watching and tweeting per day. Apparently, running the country and taking down a viciously powerful global cabal of Evil Doers doesn't take much time at all. Well, he has assured us he is "really smart" and a "stable genius," so this must be the proof.

The Storm (or something to that effect: mass arrests, uprisings, imposition of martial law, etc.) has been announced as imminent by Q multiple times, but has yet to actually materialize. Which I would argue is a very good thing, since the dreams of Q-oids sound fascistic and totally un-American to many, yours truly included.

In the broader sense, take any and all crazy, totally irresponsible, scurrilous, slanderous, outrageous claims you've ever heard anyone ever make, jumble them all together, add in baby mills, Satanism and human sacrifice, and then attribute it all to liberals—yes, bleeding heart liberals—and you now have QAnon in a nutshell.

I mean, I freely subscribe to the "conspiracy theory" which says Democrats (aka liberals), as a group, are completely incompetent. It's about the only "conspiracy" this group is traditionally capable of being a part of. The recent results of the 2018 midterms notwithstanding, the modern Dem Party has a stunning track record of snatching defeat from the jaws of victory. Witness the election that not only gave us the Man-Baby, but which put the GOP in charge of entire regions of the nation.

In summary, QAnon is, at best, an extremely dubious set of outrageous, unproven, slanderous "proofs" which, by the very nature of their delivery, are open to interpretation. Further, because many of them are so vague and ambiguous, it is relatively easy to make them align with known events, thereby providing "proof" for those who don't think too hard or delve too deeply into how ridiculous it all is.

You've probably searched the Internet and haven't found a reliable source that can answer your questions. There is no need to look any further; here you will find answers to your questions, in an orderly manner, and for beginners who have no idea about QAnon.

INTRODUCTION

Do not wait any longer, and keep reading, here we will teach you everything you need to discover and follow Q posts, and how to learn to read them. Thanks to the simple structure of the book, you will see that it helps you little by little to understand more deeply everything that surrounds us, and to realize that not everything is what it seems. You will learn to look at yourself critically.

1
WHO IS Q AND WHAT THE HELL IS THE QANON MOVEMENT?

In the fast-paced modern world of the 21st century, paranoia and conspiracy theories are widely accepted and spread like wildfire regardless of whether they are political or religion-based. Over the last few decades, researchers and political scientists have observed a pattern to conspiracy theories, i.e., they always arise whenever there's political or religious or any other kind of uncertainty about events going around in the world. And it's not a surprise that they have existed as long as humankind has existed owing to Homo sapiens' divisive nature. This relates to basic human nature. However, there are certain types of individuals who are socially more prone to such conspiratorial thinking than others. In addition, conspiracy theories have positive as well as negative impacts on society at large. On the one hand, they promote healthy cynicism. But, on the other, they equally damage the public's trust in higher authorities. Furthermore, social networking platforms also make it worse for the spread of skepticism and mass hysteria among the nations.

Therefore, this book contains everything you need to know generally about conspiracy theories and specifically about the now extremely popular and the ever-growing QAnon movement. We will shed some light on the biggest conspiracy theories that have stood the test of time and still have followers from 9/11 to moon landing to John F. Kennedy's alleged assignation. Moreover, we will expand on the basic premise of such theories, their long history, and the reasons behind them. Then, we'll discuss QAnon's origin, what sites are involved, the mystery around their identity, what they stand for, and how they communicate through their complicated methods of decoding "Q breadcrumbs." Also, the book explores the astounding role of apps like Twitter, YouTube, and Facebook in expanding and continuing the great paranoia in the political realm. And finally, there will be detailed explanations for the four biggest conspiracy theories championed by QAnon adherents.

WHO IS Q?

Q is an anonymous online group that utilizes a common language including one to describe the organizational layers of participants and the different actions they perform, and the issues they campaign for and the enemies they want to battle against. Q works at various stages, with core, acts limited to the fairly negligible user-generated 8Chan imageboard forum, while activities hit a wider range of (prospective) followers on Facebook. More precisely, Q is considered to be a high-ranking person or a select number of persons often with Q clearance working in Trump's government, a point at which highly classified and limited details can be obtained. Q stated to be a high-level intelligence informant with Q certification (hence the name) charged with uploading intelligence drops — which he named "crumbs" for whatever reason — straight to 4chan to covertly warn the public regarding POTUS' master plot to stage a counter-coup toward deep-state leaders. In brief, it was totally crazy. However, due to some very awkward occurrences — like Q sort of, kind of predicting that Trump should tweet the term "small" on Local enterprise Saturday, and this time the internet agreed that Q was "totally on Air Force One" because he shared a blurry image of some islands when Trump was still on his visit to Asia — and a whole lot of other wild speculation, people assumed he was the real deal.

While Q blogs discretely, there are signs as to who Q could be. In most breadcrumbs, the signoff as "Q" started in a message on 2 November, 2017. Prior to this point, Q had proposed the idea of a "Q Clearance." "Q Clearance" is a top-secret clearance classification for somebody who has exposure to Top Classified, Classified, and Previously Limited Records, as well as National safety Details.

I. QANON DECODED - THE AWAKENING BEGINS

The classification is comparable to the defense dept.'s Highest Security classification. However, it is necessary to remember that Q neither appears to get the specific approval, nor to operate for the Energy ministry. That is a misperception. The "Q Clearance" literally implies Q has a high-level authorization tag, which refers to the "Q Clearance" provided to Jack Ryan in a movie that he did not have the requisite authorization to help in the quest for the fugitive submarine.

The allusion to "Q clearance" is clearly intended to suggest that Q has the requisite security clearance to be able to cryptically reveal sensitive knowledge without leaks, thus protecting national defense. Q's usage of mainstream culture allusions has a dual objective: not just to preserve national stability but also as a means to reveal, mimic and thereby combat the concerted creation of pop culture through advertising by the entertainment and media industries.

Q even listed "WH," "4, 10, 20," "Q+," "Q, DELTA," and "Q [auth478-24zgP]" under several signatures. Rarely Q doesn't include a signature, but Anons realize it is Q because of the trip-code. Although hypotheses on the significance of any of these signoffs remain unconfirmed, individuals remain advised to use the signoffs inside the background of the actual articles where they occur and make their own choice.

Q stated, "We operate at the President's convenience," suggesting not just that Q is operating for Donald trump and that Q is a squad. Q used "I" a couple of times prematurely on but nowadays just uses "we" Q sometimes shares photos of the President's pen and signs, Air Force One scenes as he is flying, and other photos among crumbs that often suggest that Q is loyal to the Administration.

Q also said, "Less than ten people can verify [who or what Q is]," adding, "Only three members are civilians." It should be observed that the Board's Anons are urged not to attempt to locate or to identify who Q is. The assumption, though, is that Q is a squad of high-ranking Trump admin officials that are sharing details to awaken the public to critical and significant incidents or "happenings" that might or may not be covered by the newspapers and to have insider background. While less than ten individuals will confirm the identity of Q, it is generally accepted that there may be numerous people posting as Q. Therefore, it is normal to allude to Q as a collective noun owing to the assumption that Anons do not realize if Q is one individual or many while writing.

Whoever Q might be, photos are shared referring to a link with Q and Donald Trump, and reports are published in real-time regarding initiatives promoted by President Trump, activities he engages in, and tactics he deploys. Anons interpret Q's coded tweets in real-time, too, to seek to better grasp what the plans of President Trump were about a particular strategy or case.

There are a few Q posts signed 'Q,' and some marked Q+ is not obvious. Many (> 50) devoted YouTube Q users assume that John F Kennedy Junior is one of the Q profiles. Any Q analysts have suggested that Q+ is US President Donald Trump.

HOW DID QANON START?

QAnon is a right-wing conspiracy theory outlining a possible hidden scheme against the United States by a supposed "deep state" that is working against President Trump and the followers. This latest hypothesis of paranoia dubbed "The Storm" has invaded the darkest areas of the world. Like Pizza gate, the Storm plot includes underground cabals, an underage skin trading operation driven (partially) by the occult Democrat party, and, of course, endless conceptual leaps and unfounded conclusions that refuse to stand up against the most reality-based scrutiny; Unlike Pizza-gate, though, the Crisis is not based on a particular block of DC shops, or communications from John Podesta. Its size is a lot larger than just that.

The QAnon concept (also alluded to as 'Q') was born on 28 October 2017. A first message on the 4Chan internet chat forum by anonymous poster ID "gb953qGI" emerged on the /pol/ site. But the author is not listed by this initiating post as 'Q.' This tale started with a message on /pol/, a sub-message board of the 4chan forum. In the past couple of years, /pol/ — which literally stands for "politically incorrect" — gradually but steadily has been a strong candidate for the ever-elusive designation of the most unsettling online culture. p It's the kind of place simply where neo-Nazis and number of people who believe that women shouldn't have fundamental rights used to connect before people started checking them out on

I. QANON DECODED - THE AWAKENING BEGINS

Twitter and electing a president them to public office. And as of late, its ranks have been expanded to include lunatic participants of all various types.

The hypothesis started in October 2017 with an unsettling 4-channel post called 'Calm before the Storm" posted by someone named 'Q Clearance Nationalist.'

The first crumb Q shared was on 4chan, an online web picture board founded in 2003. Q was first published on the forum of /pol/ on the thread called "Mueller Probe" on 28 October 2017, and on other forums until 31 October 2017, Q was posted on the thread entitled "Food Crumbs-Q Clearance Nationalist." The thread "Calm before the Storm" (CBTS), titled after the perplexing word spoken by President Trump on 5 October 2017, was generated on 1 November 2017. Q posted on numerous CBTS iterations (536 threads) before reporting that 4Chan was hacked and protection breached, prompting a switch to 8Chan to maintain Q's credibility guaranteed to readers.

In 2013, 8chan, an un-affiliated 4chan-like picture forum, was introduced as a free-speaking response to the 4chan censorship. On 19 November 2017, a forum was generated with the same title as the Q thread posted in on 4chan /cbts/. Q wrote on /CBTS/ until 6 January 2018 (308 general threads in total), reporting that the board had been infiltrated as well. Q had trouble utilizing, among other cases, the trip-code, a registration code that confirms the identification of a user, especially on 14 and 21 December 2017. This failure to use the trip-code obliged Anons to build a new message board: /the storm/. Q first reported 5 January 2018, on /the storm/. After 41 generic threads, Q and Anons quit accessing /the storm/ because of internal conflicts and personal-promotion, prompting a move to another new forum.

Then the platform, still in use today, was produced on Monday, 8 January 2018, called /qresearch/, which must then be referred to as "The Board." After that point, Q has also been able to upload openly on that message board, and keeps posting crumbs until the time it was published. On 8 January 2018, Q also built a private forum for Q to post in alone, called /greatawakening/. Q started using /greatawakening/ on 28 March, 2018, saying she was under threat. Eventually, after a postponement, on 4 May,

2018, Q created /patriotsfight/, the secret board Q uses today. Q has shared crumbs on both of these forums that can be addressed by Anons on /qresearch/ with Q, but any new to The Forum are advised to first study how Anons function and research before they participate.

He claimed the pizzeria was part of a sex ring with girls, a scheme known as Pizzagate. Theorists on Reddit and 4chan reported that readers could discover a child sex network in John Podesta's stolen emails — if only one were to swap terms like "pizza" with "tiny kid." 8 months later, a guy going by "Q" first reported on 4chan's unofficial political message board, among the most controversial and radical locations on the web — and a hotbed of discussion. Even Q's first article had been littered with typical theories that had never existed. This was the beginning of the QAnon hypothesis that has built on a few ideas that have sparked Pizzagate.

2
THE MAIN THEORIES OF Q'S IDENTITY, IS TRUMP INVOLVED?

Just how close is Q to the president of the United States? Besides the picture proof of him riding in the airplane with the president, there are some other instances where Q seemed to be able to influence Trump.

For example, one Anon contacted Q and asked him to have the president use the phrase "tip top into one of Trump's many speeches. This was so that they can verify if Q indeed had pulled on the leader and also to serve as a confirmation to the QAnon members that Trump is acknowledging them. Sure enough, in the president's address during a White House event, the Easter Egg Roll, Trump said that the White House is in "tippy top" shape.

It was also used in another speech that the president made where he was asking for "tip top" nuclear arsenal. After the speeches, Q posted the message that the request has been relayed to the president. He also asked if the QAnon readers listened to the president's speech. Coincidence? It could be but it still caused a lot of individuals to start believing that Q really had the president's ear.

Another well-analyzed instance where there seemed to be a connection with President Trump and QAnon was when Q posted several cryptic phrases, "Safety & Security" and "Catch & Release".

Afterward, President Trump posted a tweet on Twitter thanking the National Border Patrol Council's Brandon Judd for showing how badly the country needs the wall that he has been lobbying for from the very beginning of his administration.

The president included that measures must be taken in order to stop the loophole known as "catch & release" as well as clean up procedures of processes at the border for reasons of "safety & security". The use of the keywords released by Q was viewed by the QAnon members that Trump is indeed connected to Q and that he is secretly communication with them. Letting them know that he knows they are there.

Another, albeit flimsy, example of Trump's covert acknowledgment that the QAnon movement exists was featured during one of his interviews. There, he was talking about how he came to choose to become the US President. He mentioned that he visited Washington, D.C. about 17 times. The president repeated that statement several times. This number is significant to the followers of Q because the 17th letter of the alphabet just happens to be the letter Q. It was said that Trump was signaling the members that he knows they are out there.

If the posts of Q were indeed real, then this could indicate that the current administration has found an alternative channel by which they can communicate with their supporters, bypassing the traditional news outlets and even social media. This makes sense because Trump is not secretive of his dislike for mainstream media. He views them as the enemy. This channel is more direct. People think that if Trump has something to say to his supporters, he would need somebody like Q in order to reach them without alerting the people that are opposing him.

Another point of legitimacy is that the administration has yet to confirm nor deny if the movement is indeed true. If it were not valid, the government would have spoken up by now in order to distance itself from a false channel. That is how many choose to justify the continuing existence of Q.

What the palace has done though is indirectly denounce groups that encourage others to do violent acts. This was established during an interview with Sara Huckabee Sanders, the White House press secretary, following the incident of hecklers harassing CNN's Jim Acosta.

I. QANON DECODED- THE AWAKENING BEGINS

When she was asked whether the president supports the QAnon group, she simply stated that the president doesn't condone any group that will incite any form of violence against another individual. She added that the president definitely doesn't support any organization that supports and promotes that type of behavior towards others.

While this may seem like a blow to QAnon, some individuals see this as encouraging. They claimed that the president is distancing himself from the group so that they can remain safe. If the public, and Deep State, knew that the president supports a group, its members could be put in danger. The followers believe that by publicly denouncing QAnon, the president is only protecting them. Still a lot of them believe that the president knows about the existence of the QAnon movement.

This is not the first time that government agencies have used alternative channels to send out communication. Back in the days of the first Cold War, the British and American spies would occasionally send coded messages placed in the classified ads of newspapers in order to talk to each other. The NSA was reported to be doing an updated version of this tactic.

Instead of using newspapers, they opted to utilize the group's public Twitter account in order to communicate with a potential source from Russia. This is just one small detail of this scandalous interaction. According to reports, CIA and NSA agents have traveled to Germany in order to try to recover certain pieces of cyberweapons that have been stolen from the intelligence agencies of America.

A spy from Russia supposedly offered the pilfered cyber tools back to the US in exchange for a whopping $10 million. The US agents eventually managed to have the price lowered to just a million dollars. The spy even offered up shocking information about President Trump. It was not determined whether the intelligence officers from the United States paid for the information that the spy was selling in addition to the cyber tools that were repurchased.

Based on the article, this unnamed Russian spy was able to meet in Germany with the US agents. In order to arrange the meeting and work out the details of their exchange, the NSA sent missives to the Russian spy using coded messages posted on their Twitter account. Some asked if the messages were sent directly or were, they posted in public.

According to James Risen, a writer from The Intercept, the messages were very much public. The tweet appeared completely benign but it contained hidden information that only the American and Russian spies understood. NSA has reached out to various media channels to deny that it has been sending coded messages.

What is most troubling about this issue was not that the US intelligence agencies seemed keen on purchasing intelligence that could be bad for President Trump. This includes an alleged videotape of the president having relations with a sex worker recorded back in 2013. This will probably be met with indifference.

What is surprising is that these agencies have become so brazen that they are sending messages in plain sight. Their tweets are so public that no one would think to look further into what has been posted. No one except for the keen-eyed members of the QAnon movement.

Of course, when you are labeled a theorist, nobody would really pay attention to what you are saying, no matter how valid or true your message is.

Many individuals who have been keeping track of the social media posts of various government agencies have been labeled as theorists. This term is so dismissive that no matter what proof you present, nobody would believe you. Worse, these "theorists" are ridiculed and asked where their foil hats are. If a government agency tweets a certain date or a number, many theorists try to find connections to existing events. These get laughed at by most for being absurd. And then their paranoia gets vindicated when these types of revelations occur.

Many of the members of the QAnon movement are still waiting for their, "I told you so" moment. Once Q's prophecies finally come to fruition, these people will finally be "vindicated" for believing something that seemed so convolutedly harebrained. When the time comes, it is not just the QAnon followers who will win. They say that everybody wins because then, Deep State will be no more.

I. QANON DECODED - THE AWAKENING BEGINS

THE STIRRINGS OF THE QANON MOVEMENT

During rallies, it is common to see people holding up signs for others to read. As people watched the news coverage on one of President Trump's rally to campaign for Republican Representative Ron DeSantis in Florida, they noticed something peculiar. Instead of the familiar "Trump 2020" and "Women for Trump" signs, a new one has cropped up.

In the crowd, signs saying "We are Q" were held up by various individuals. Some journalists also noted that a number of people in the audience were wearing t-shirts with the word "QAnon" in the front. Yet another held a cryptic message stating "Q WWG1WGA" with a kicker of "Keep America Great!". These were followed by signs stating that mainstream media is the enemy. What was this group about? Some people thought that it was an organization that is working to promote Trump. While this may be true, the group of Qs is more than that.

These placards and shirts refer to a growing movement that is increasingly becoming popular particularly among those that belong to the far-right group. The entire movement, if it can be called that, has been called a "conspiracy cult" and "a grassroots movement" that is slowly exposing the hidden battles between President Trump and the Deep State.

QAnon is a shifting and growing theory that began as an ultra-fringe concept posted on the online message boards. These sites were frequented by alt-right members. Now that it has gotten bigger and its reach has widened, their messages are now available on mainstream platforms such as Reddit, YouTube, Facebook, and Twitter.

The movement's beliefs are anchored on the assertion that Trump is an all-seeing, omnipotent entity. Their main theory is that President Trump has been selected in order to bring back goodness into this world. That he is only acting like a buffoon and seemed to be making so many mistakes to prevent his enemies from realizing what a genius he really is.

For example, when the Mueller inquiry was instigated, it was said to be an investigation to establish if the Trump campaign indeed colluded with the Russian government. According to QAnon beliefs, this is just a charade of sorts.

Q followers believe that Trump controlled the Mueller investigation in order to target certain individuals belonging to the Democratic party, as well as a few Hollywood names, for their involvement with the Deep state, sex rings, and other controversial and illegal activities. It also implicates huge pharmaceutical companies for taking part in activities that are meant to keep the American people drugged and unaware.

Members of QAnon believe that there is a certain individual, Q, who is slowly but surely revealing the extent of the plot. Each revelation is said to be confirmed by parsing selected parts of the president's public speeches. The term that Q believers use for this movement is "the Great Awakening".

While some view this awakening as the revealing of the true nature of people who used to be honored for what was perceived as their contributions to the world, others say that the awakening is the "opening of the eyes" of the masses. The awakening is the unveiling of all the lies that used to be taken as gospel truth.

Leading this awakening is President Trump. He is using the US military and the National Security Agency in order to wage a secret war against the powerful globalists. Another part of the awakening is the restoration of Reaganite family values in America.

QAnon members see this war literally as the ultimate battle between evil and good. And the Awakening is just the beginning. They believe that ones the evil has been dispersed and all that are responsible are already in jail, Trump will take the next step to make the country even greater than it is now.

3
THE GLOBAL AWAKENING: THE FIGHT AGAINST THE EVIL

As a matter of record for now and the future, presents Q, the president, and the QAnon group in a straightforward way.

Without them, the Great Awakening would never have begun, and we would not now be seeing it grow into what the evidence suggests is literally a Global Awakening.

And I do mean global, because in my extensive research I have seen pictures and comments and articles about Q from many countries outside America. Clearly, the Great Awakening as it is called in the United States is far more than simply an American aberration.

From New Zealand in the deep south Pacific through Australia and South America (Ecuador for instance) and Japan and Hong Kong and on to the UK and Europe, there is much evidence of a great unrest, and a rising tide of opposition to the reign and rule of the Globalists.

In France, and elsewhere in Europe at least 43 straight weekends of demonstrations by those calling themselves Yellow Jackets is but one example of how the Illuminati spider web is being torn apart, strand by strand.

The "Brexit" referendum in the UK that saw the majority vote to leave the European Union, which was established by the elite as part of their

One World Government plan, is further evidence that a Great Awakening is underway.

Yet no more clearly is this seen than in the United States, where the election of Donald Trump as president and then the appearance of Q on the Internet has resulted in a storm like no other in history.

President Trump spoke of "the calm before the storm" shortly after his inauguration, That calm has long since gone, replaced by virulent opposition to his occupation of the White House and ever-increasing efforts to have him unseated, because having told the world (at the United Nations) that America rejects Globalism, he served notice that the days of the Deep State are numbered.

Worldwide Network

The Deep State is not just a few rogue elements in America's government (on both sides of the House) or a few conspirators in the Intelligence and Justice agencies. The Deep State also has its proponents in the vast worldwide network of companies, banks and international corporations.

They are fighting for their very existence, and in some cases, for their lives, using every dirty trick in their playbook to destroy the president - which is why they are hell-bent on also destroying the QAnon movement and with it, the Great Awakening.

Admittedly, many people, perhaps in the hundreds of thousands, or even in the millions, will buy into the media campaign to convince them that QAnons are nothing but radical members of a cult, peddling a conspiracy theory. But many others will want to work it out for themselves, perhaps thinking, "if only 10 percent of what the QAnons talk about is valid, or perhaps 25 or 30%, is it really a conspiracy at all?" Such individuals may then deduce that to call someone a conspiracy theorist is to intentionally and deliberately attack the messenger in order to divert attention from the message. It has worked throughout history. Until now.

And that is why we are faced with a future that will see this storm continue to disrupt the very fabric of society, just as a real hurricane initially forms in calm waters, gathers strength and movement, and cuts a swathe of destruction through everything in its path, leaving a trail of debris in its wake, wherein the survivors, especially those who had been

1. QANON DECODED - THE AWAKENING BEGINS

aware of what was coming and took steps to plan accordingly, must pick up the pieces and start afresh.

It is that imagery that has seen hundreds of individuals become citizen journalists and investigators, creating YouTube video channels and newsletters and blogs that little by little and piece by piece combine to alert others as to what is gathering strength - "The Storm" as it is called - as well as what to expect, and how to prepare.

Among them is British computer scientist and writer, Martin Geddes.

By no means would I classify him as a Q "follower," any more than I am. But we are both objectively aware of Q and the QAnon movement. In my case, I am a reporter of current events, focusing on those who are having a very severe impact on American and world society. Mr. Geddes' essays cover a wide variety of topics, and his Twitter presence has attracted something like 63,000 followers.

We have corresponded through a brief series of emails, because two of his essays in particular caught my eye when I came across his Internet presence while researching the global impact of President Trump's hard line against the Deep State and its worldwide influence.

As Martin said in one of his emails, "To discredit the messenger in order to distract from the message is core to Q's construction: the messenger [in this case, Q] is a will-o'-the-wisp, an apparition, a virtual avatar - with no body, history, identity to attack."

True, they have no individual to attack, but their constant debunking of the QAnon movement as a whole, is evidence that they do read the Q posts and discussion boards, and they are terminally afraid of the Great and Global Awakening.

The Big Question

That is also why they have so far refused to ask President Trump "are you associated with the QAnon conspiracy in any way Mr. President?"

Just imagine if he were to say "I'm aware of it. And yes, these QAnons are patriots - Republicans and Democrats and Independents who think for themselves. Q tells them what the Fake News refuses to tell them - the truth about the real conspiracies."

MR. BABYLON

No doubt that looks like a fantasy scenario, but at some point, someone will ask that question; perhaps it will be a "Q friendly" reporter, possibly even an individual who was deliberately inserted into the media world long ago as a wide- awake "sleeper" waiting to act when the time is right.

Fantasy or not, the reality is that Q's many posts since 2017 have focused with amazing accuracy on exposing the many evil doings of the Deep State and its multiple adherents among US politicians and government agencies.

Q has also frequently exhorted us to think for ourselves, to do our own research, to think logically rather than emotionally, objectively rather than subjectively.

In other words, there is wisdom in being both contemplative, and analytical, which I believe is so very well illustrated in this following essay by Martin Geddes.

❈ 4 ❈
THE DEEP STATE: A SECRET PLAN TO GOVERN THE WORLD

In one of the drops, Q lists the three main puppet masters as the House of Saud, the Rothschild family and George Soros. Let's take a few moments to understand why Q would be compelled to communicate this information to the movement.

The House of Saud

The constitution says We the People have the power but it doesn't always feel like that. Q suggests three main puppet masters are pulling the strings that hold us in place. These puppet masters use their money, power and influence to impose a New World Order and the world is fighting back. Q has devoted many messages to exposing numerous current and ongoing operations taking place to combat the puppet masters.

Saudi Crown Prince Mohammed bin Salman aka (MbS) is responsible for the purge and an ambitious reform plan to modernize Saudi Arabia. Despite the controversy surrounding the death of a Saudi reporter, MbS and President Trump have remained close allies and it appears the west has a strategic partner in the region.

The Rothschild Family

Rothschild is the lord and master of the money markets of the world and virtually lord and master of everything else.

MR. BABYLON

- Benjamin Disraeli

The Rothschild legacy goes back hundreds of years to a wise father who instructed his sons to work amongst each other to create lasting family wealth. Unlike other families who develop bonds with one particular country, the brothers operated in different European nations but they shared news and information to become Europe's most powerful institution. From the 19th century to today, every war and most grand infrastructure projects required a loan and someone from the Rothschild family was willing to finance the effort.

It's one thing to finance a home or a car or even a college degree, financing a nation is a completely different exercise. If a debtor fails to pay back the loan, you can take back the house or car but owning a nation's debt creates a lot of leverage. The Rothschild's made their business by making loans to Western European powers. When loaning money no one can guarantee 100% loan repayment and national creditworthiness is essential for a functional government. So, how do you believe the Rothschild family is treated by the people responsible for controlling the national purse strings supplied via Rothschild loans? Owning national debt creates an international get out of jail free card and a seemingly endless amount on actionable financial information.

For example, the country of Brazil was created thanks in part to Nathan Rothschild who negotiated a loan that financed Brazilian independence from Portugal. The Portuguese government had borrowed money from a Rothschild bank earlier but stopped debt repayment. With his knowledge of Portugal's economic issues and existing relationships with the would-be Brazilian government, Nathan used Brazilian independence to transfer Portugal's debt to the newly established Brazilian government. Soon after, a Rothschild bank financed Brazil's new debt (Portugal's old debt) with another loan which basically created several income streams from one initial loan. It's hard to say how much Portuguese and Brazilian families benefited from the original loans though it's easy to see how the Rothschild family enriched themselves at the expense of ordinary citizens.

Several movies and books exist related to the Rothschild story though no one has been able to deliver the definitive account. I honestly don't know the extent of collaboration between the Rothschild family and national governments but I believe there's much to learn concerning how this family has been able to exert global influence for almost 200 years.

George Soros

The third puppet master was born in Budapest and emigrated to England after World War II, George Soros and his Open Society Foundation have been linked to government destabilization in Europe. Soros has been open in his support of liberal and progressive international agendas.

Malaysian Prime Minister Mahathir Mohamad believes Soros is responsible for a speculative attack on Southeast Asia's currencies which erased 15% of the value of the Malaysian currency in 1997. Mahatir was quoted on his feelings toward Soros's intervention, "Attempting to starve an entire country so as to drive its administration to carry on, that isn't our thought. In the event that you need to act against the administration, you act against the government.... You need to give them that the manner in which others do things can carry advantages to the nation without in any capacity sabotaging their position."

It's obvious that Soros believes his wealth gives him the right to make decisions that impact a sovereign nation's ability to rule its citizens. Fed up with the constant criticism flowing from the Soros founded Central European University (CEU), Turkish Prime Minister Viktor Orban endorsed a law passed by Hungary's Parliament that would force the university to close if it did not open an American campus. After several years of legal battles and controversies, CEU was forced to move its campus from Budapest to Vienna. In addition, Prime Minister Orban has targeted Soros with a new law that made "promoting and supporting illegal migration" a criminal offense subject to 12 months in prison.

Q's first message in October 2017 suggested that we follow the money after Soros donated $18 billion. It's clear that the global power elite does not have the best interests of all at heart so we have to unite ourselves to overcome their plan of oppression. Building with other patriots is the only way to defeat the puppet masters.

MR. BABYLON

WHO HAS THE KNOWLEDGE?

I don't know about Cryptocurrency and I'm unquestionably not a specialist but rather I comprehend why individuals are amped up for the thought and others are dreadful. At present, Central Banks control the progression of cash for a large portion of the world which implies under 1,000 individuals decide the amount of the world goes through cash. The banks have made the case that their framework is the best way to trade esteem. Numerous individuals accept this to be valid and that conviction makes Central Banks incredibly amazing. Regardless of whether it's in reality evident or not isn't as significant as the conviction held by millions. Cryptographic money gives an option in contrast to the present framework which subverts the need of a Central Bank and the conviction of millions. People are just constrained by their convictions. In this way, making an elective framework for all intents and purposes takes out the requirement for Central Banks and the force that originates from controlling most budgetary exchanges. We realize that force undermines and this is apparent in the decisions made by the Central Banks.

Presently, we have a gathering of youthful progressives asserting that these Central Banks are not, at this point essential for individuals to trade esteem. Cryptographic money, as most things on the web, works admirably of dispensing with the go between. Cash is traded starting with one individual then onto the next without conventional bank association. The exchange is enlisted through a procedure called the Blockchain which comprises of numerous PCs checking scrambled pieces of the message. Decentralizing this data takes out the requirement for the Central Banks and liberates people to trade cash without outside obstruction.

DISENTANGLING THE MESSAGE

QAnon works similarly as the Blockchain. When Q sends the drops, a great many people are dealing with their own to disentangle the message. No one is relied upon to know it all, that is an inconceivable objective. In any case, when the full intensity of QAnon is applied as a powerful influence for a specific issue or question, that is the point at which the enchantment occurs. The gathering joins to share data while working together on subsequent stages. Despite the fact that there is anything but an accepted pioneer, it's stunning to perceive how sorted out the development truly is.

In case you're thinking about turning into a piece of the Great Awakening, simply realize that you aren't relied upon to know it all on Day #1. You are relied upon to tune in to and not simply hear the messages being conveyed. Acumen is vital and explore is empowered. Verbal looseness of the bowels isn't to anybody's greatest advantage, it's increasingly viable to assess all accessible data and procedure the realities before letting free an undigested information dump. We include nationalists inside the development who have devoted their lives to instructing the majority, use them an asset and notice their advice. By perusing this book, you will have a superior comprehension of how to reveal the insider facts in Q's messages and where to search for direction when you're befuddled about what to do straightaway. You can't know it all however you should realize where to look.

At long last, you are the response to the inquiry. The thought behind QAnon is by all accounts about shielding the nation from Deep State entertainers who are plotting to oust the legislature. You can't take care of an issue that you didn't know existed, mindfulness. You can't take care of a difficult you don't get, examine. Most extraordinary issues can't be comprehended alone, join together. Where we go one, we go all (WWG1WGA)

THE MOST POPULAR Q'S PREDICTIONS I

The issue that QAnon models for the Trump machinery is that when they can pull in media consideration at Trump occasions, it conveys a message that pieces of his base are separated from the real world — and gives Democrats a conceivable weapon to use against Trump.

Over the previous year, increasingly more QAnon fans who likewise bolster Trump have claimed that their Q apparatus and shirts have been restricted from the president's assemblies, and they have blamed security faculty for teaching them to, for example, turn their T-shirts back to front. The secret service of the U.S. as well as intelligence, for its part has freely denied that it is associated with QAnon concealment at Trump rallies. On the off chance that QAnon-related dress and signs are prohibited, it's conceivable that the boycott has been forced by extra, procured security monitors, as opposed to the Secret Service.

A year ago, ecstatic Trump by one way or another wound up posturing for an Oval Office photograph operation with YouTube intrigue scholar Lionel Lebron, one of the main advertisers of the QAnon hypothesis. In July, Trump welcomed a few QAnon advertisers to his White House Social Media Summit, where he applauded the QAnon pushers and other "meme smiths" for their work for his sake.

I. QANON DECODED - THE AWAKENING BEGINS

Trump's invitees included professional Trump web character Bill Mitchell, who has advanced QAnon on Twitter, and artist Joy Villa, who wore "Q" studs to the Conservative Political Action Conference. Another QAnon-pushing invitee, visual artist Ben Garrison, was removed from the list of attendees at last on account of the tumult over an enemy of Semitic animation he had made.

Q adherents have depended on unconventional specialty strategies to get around the evident restriction on QAnon gear at Trump rallies. Some of the time, they spread QAnon shirts with another shirt to get past security, at that point take off the distraction shirt once the assembly begins. In August, Trump's election campaign advertisement highlighted, obviously incidentally, numerous authorized crusade signs that had been doctored with tape and markers to demonstrate "Q's."

Some QAnon devotees have even begun pursuing a position. Two GOP House applicants have said they trust in the notion, which could attach Republicans further to the QAnon periphery if those up-and-comers win their primaries.

The nearness of Q adherents at assemblies additionally means Trump could unintentionally underwrite the hypothesis, at any rate according to its devotees. About each Trump appearance produces film that QAnon devotees investigate in order to see Trump's hand developments structure what they accept to be a "Q."

The White House has recently released a transcript of telephonic conversation between President Donald Trump and his Ukrainian counterpart Volodymyr Zelensky. As indicated by the archive, Trump asked Zelensky to do him "some help" and research the roots of the Russia probe just as previous VP Joe Biden.

For a considerable length of time the Americans tilted on the far right relied upon suspected theories to clarify the reasons underlying the country's inclination in embracing dynamic arrangements of which they object.

Trump is currently reinitiating and dealing with a conception that began after he took his political decision, yet it was up to the periphery components on privilege whereas, to a great extent disregarded. That is the conviction which is used by U.S. President's adversaries, majority of them

MR. BABYLON

being raised by the staunch supporters of Barack Obama and Hilary Clinton, while the rest of it coming from those occupying significant executive slots in different offices, utilizing situations for gradually embracing a rebellion, intended to expel from power the lawfully chosen president and obliterate his organization.

Former NSA spy Edward Snowden has utilized the term deep state by and large to allude to the impact of government employees over chosen authorities. According to him, deep state does not only revolve around espionage institutions, it impliedly talks about bureaucracy working under the executive branch. These include authority members who are occupying top government slots, who keep a close eye on President round the clock. They tend to go back and forth. By impacting the approach...... They impact President.

As per political specialist George Friedman, the Deep State, established in 1871, proceeds underneath the government, controlling and much of the time reshaping approaches; In this view, civil service of U.S. was made to constrain the intensity of the president. Before 1871, the president could choose government workers, each and every one those who served the administration upon insistence of the President. However, the situation has now changed and dynamics are different

Michael Crowley, senior diplomatic reporter for Politico expressed, "Underneath the legislative issues of comfort, lies the reality that an enormous portion of the United States government truly operates in the absence of straightforwardness or open investigation, and has manhandled its marvelous powers in a bunch of ways."

Educator Royce Lindsey is of the view if we take constitutional plan out of picture, deep state conception valuable to comprehend parts of security situation foundation in created nations, alongside highlighting it in the context of United States. Lindsey suggests that the covert government solicits power from intelligence institutions as well as those of national security. Overall, the concept is viewed as utterly mysterious.

Following the exposure of records discharged by international non-profit organization WikiLeaks, this terminology was embraced by individuals who claimed that the data focuses on covert government connivance which goes onto subvert majority rules system the strategic objectives of "the individuals"

Journalist Lee Smith wrote a book by the name of, "The Plot against The President" In this book, he writes that the prevalent idea in society is that Russia subverted popularity-based procedures during the 2016 election, the genuine harm was done not by Moscow or some other remote on-screen character. Or maybe, this was a moderate move of overthrow designed by a cadre of the American tip top, the 'secret government,' focusing on the president, yet additionally the remainder of the nation

On the off chance that you calmly pursue American legislative issues, these appear rather uncontroversial articulations. Yet, in case you're a bad-to-the-bone supporter of President Donald Trump, you may have had questions about some of them before.

That is on the grounds that Trump drove fear inspired notions about Obama's origin, Cruz's dad and Scalia's demise for political bit of leeway previously and during the 2016 presidential political decision, and when every hypothesis outlasted its convenience, he proceeded onward. In any case, the harm he exacted in empowering this sort of reasoning has now saturated legislative issues such that won't be anything but difficult to kill.

As President, Trump has proceeded with a similar example of conduct. At the point when MSNBC have Joe Scarborough turned out to be progressively incredulous of Trump reporting in real time, the President tweeted out a fear inspired notion about him. At the point when a mystery recording of Trump talking about satisfying previous Playboy model Karen McDougal surfaced, the President indicated that it may have been altered to make him look awful.

It's misty if anything Trump could do, regardless of whether he needed, to pack down the theory, since any refusal could simply be deciphered by its supporters as a major aspect of the all-inclusive strategy.

The majority of this is going on when Americans are more defenseless against disinformation than any time in recent memory.

Online life stages like Twitter, YouTube and Facebook have turned out to be tremendously incredible pieces of the data biological system, making them focuses for everybody from web trolls to dishonesty divided hacks to Russian insight operators trying to plant disagreement.

In any case, at a central level, such a large number of us basically need to accept fear inspired notions. They help us discover significance in the bedlam of the day by day news; promise us that somebody is in control — regardless of whether that is a saint or a reprobate who could be crushed — as opposed to a variety of generic powers;

In that capacity, a postmodern administration fits assessment and contestation identified with open organization. The postmodern condition in open organization requires an alternate sort of establishment to comprehend the new talks developing to control (or not) approach and practice. In particular, the inquiry presented here is: How does the postmodern condition influence managerial morals?

This is notwithstanding government workers setting up a system of informal "opposition" or "rebel" online networking records to challenge President Trump's conclusions and activities encompassing environmental change inquire about.

Clearly, a few overseers see the president's morals as inconsistent with their own and have tested him in like manner. Nonetheless, in spite of inside analysis and opposition President Trump's conduct only from time to time changes. Rather, the president is resistant, depicting negative inclusion as "phony news", and employing paranoid fears to undermine pundits.

Eventually, regardless of whether the display is intelligent or not is far less significant than the feelings, values, bunch distinguishing pieces of proof, and representative undertones it moves. Oneself characterizing nature of the postmodern display, as performative morals, challenges advancement in light of the fact that postmodern "certainties," or (relevant to the talk) "post-certainties," are only here and there established in the goal "genuine" of innovation. The scene isn't a gathering of pictures yet a social connection among individuals interceded by pictures.

Senior White House Advisor Stephen Miller as of late asserted the indictment request jeopardizing Donald Trump's administration was a result of the "secret government". He likewise expressed in a meeting that it ought not to be paid attention to. Stephen Miller said that the informant grievance against President Trump requesting help of remote nations was associated with the deep state. "I know the difference between a whistleblower and a deep state agent," Miller said.

Republican legislators and gathering authorities, just as traditionalist media have recently been raising the theory of deep state again lately.

6
THE MOST POPULAR Q'S PREDICTIONS II

In the modern world, it is extremely easy for conspiracy theories to spread like wildfires, especially if the majority of the crowd is already cynical of the current establishment; the status quo. QAnon theories have therefore gained so much momentum in recent years since there are millions of pro-trump advocates who were ready to jump to an opportunity to support him. For starters, Republican politicians have long challenged the validity of global warming, so much so that they consider it a fraud. In this situation, when justifying skepticism of climate change, Republicanism is just as descriptive as a conspiracy theory. Yet that is not the case for hoax theories not dragged into the electoral arena, including those regarding AIDS, vaccines, and genetically altered crops. If theories like these are a platform for common religious and political figures, opinions in them may grow very quickly.

The biggest conspiracy theories that QAnon has managed to come up with and spread throughout the globe.

Pizzagate

Pizzagate is the largely discredited idea that a clandestine pedophile group operated out of a loosely linked DC pizzeria with former presidential nominee Hillary Clinton. Pizzagate is a perfect example of a fairly recent cycle of conspiracy. Since the internet will promote speculation these days

I. QANON DECODED- THE AWAKENING BEGINS

by shrinking the environment rather than expanding it: through computationally enforced echo chambers and specific topic-focused forums, living the existence in a propagandistic, entirely new world is simple. Conjecture within the Pizzagate echo-bubble (which was ever more repeated when the hypothesis advocates have booted off more traditional sites like Reddit) finally hit such a level that a claimant raced across several states to shoot shots inside the pizzeria. Luckily nobody was hurt.

Yet really, perhaps the strangest is yet to arrive. We are experiencing a full global trust crisis. Theories of hired "crisis actors" claiming to be victims of crises are nothing special — the children of color who integrate schools of little Rock, Kansas, were already suspected of being hired shills in 1957 —but nowadays the conspiracies of crisis actors accompany every strike, every uprising, every fire. It's just going to get tougher to determine what is true and what is false. Technological advances focused on artificial intelligence can exploit audio and video to replicate conversations and remarks that never existed in a smooth way. Similar engineering was leveraged to build "deep-fakes"— non-consensual porn in which the identity of a prostitute is artificially fused onto the body of a pornographic actress. It doesn't require much ingenuity to see how shills might exploit this software to propagate lies against celebrities, global leaders or, really, everyone else. Seeing photos hasn't believed for a while now so nothing would be with AI-enabled trickery.

The completely unfounded conspiracy theory suggests that Hillary Clinton and her then-campaign manager, John Podesta, oversaw a child abuse racket in the DC pizzeria basement, Comet Ping Pong (which doesn't even have a cellar). In the past few years, social media allies of Donald Trump and white nationalists have promoted the theory — contributing to stories like "Pizzagate: How 4Chan Exposed Washington's Secret Elite's Sick Universe" on false news blogs.

Pizzagate on troll refuge and discussion forum 4chan seems to have launched. After the documents from John Podesta have been leaked (probably by Russian agents) and released by Wikileaks, 4chan users find communications between Podesta and Elephantids regarding a Clinton fundraiser that occurred early in the campaign in October.

Deep State

Deep state researchers believe that the common goal of globalist organizations is to depopulate and subjugate America and all the other nations. America's domination and devastation are a central goal of the Committee of 13 and the Committee of 300. USA has the biggest armed services and market. The country is hard to conquer by coercion as it contains the greatest number of weapons possessed by people as covered under the Second Constitutional amendment of America. In the 2016 campaign the Deep State gang supported the Democrat party. This network of corruption has conspired by all means to oust Donald Trump from his Office.

The contextualization of JFK (murdered in 1963) and the alleged assassination of President Ronald Reagan in 1981 was allegedly related to an ability to neutralize influence over America through the deep state. The MSM (fake mass news media) is an important Deep State sponsor.

This deep state principle shapes the prevailing rationale for all behavior of Q. Whenever Q opens an event, in the context of this master-frame, the path in which 'work' is being taken is written. Therefore, the first step is the immediate presumption that fake reporting is fraudulent; following which the thorough evidence test will expose the actual or indirect participation of the different players in the Cartel.

COVID-19 Pandemic

Mainstream theories regarding coronavirus emerge in two types: those who question the seriousness of the virus and those who say it could be a biological weapon. The former type was actually supported by Donald Trump, who early in the pandemic referred to coronavirus as the "new hoax" of the Democrats. Indeed, even though the mortality rate rises, leftist-media figures tend to cast skepticism on the truth of the outbreak. For starters, Rush Limbaugh claimed that our leaders in public health are deep-state spies, and might even be medical authorities. The argument has been advanced by some political activists that hospitals should not necessarily handle any COVID-19 cases, reaching so far as to urge individuals to check out community hospitals and record the number of patients moving in and out.

The second form of the conspiracy theory of coronavirus argues that the virus was deliberately concocted in a laboratory by international nations, such as Russia or China, or by billionaire including George Soros and Bill

I. QANON DECODED- THE AWAKENING BEGINS

Gates: maybe China developed or experimented with this strain of coronavirus, and maybe Bill Gates and the WHO are planning to dominate the world by giving vaccines; or perhaps the virus escaped by mistake.

First there was the global epidemic, and then the "info emic" came — a word described by the head of the WHO as circulating misleading knowledge regarding COVID-19. Coronavirus related theories are the most damaging conspiracies are now component of the QAnon trend. Performers in QAnon have been downplaying the seriousness of the situation for some time now, amplifying the scientific lies and producing hoaxes.

The QAnon campaign began in 2017 when someone had previously shared insane theories regarding the US president Trump using an unofficial account named as Q on the internet platform 4chan.

In January, 2020 QAnon spread theories on 8kun (the officially recognized internet forum as 8chan), Telegram (a coded instant messaging platform) and Facebook regarding a false hypothesis that Asians were more vulnerable to coronavirus, and that white folks were resistant to COVID-19. Not only are racial undertones connected with this propaganda, but the danger presented by the disease is minimized.

From February through March 2nd week, QAnon followed Trump's lead in downplaying the virus' danger and labeling it a hoax. We claimed that the epidemic was a deep state conspiracy to destroy the prospects of re-election for the president. The QAnon group said some alert of the pandemic danger sought to distract away from US national policy, interrupt Trump protests, and erase all the economic development that they believed had arisen under Trump's presidency.

Once the WHO updated coronavirus to a pandemic level and the USA declared that it had closed its doors for 30 days to most citizens in Europe, QAnon shifted the story again. Instantly, QAnon figured the outbreak was important to rejoice as it was an excuse for the hidden plot for the Current regime to detain shadow government officers.

Under the QAnon community, Christians interpreted the outbreak as the imminent arrival of God's reign on Earth. QAnon culture influencers said that there was little need to be worried about COVID-19 in a live stream.

Hayes told his audience that they would not be harmed by the virus as this was "spiritual battle"— the virus would harm only those people which haven't been selected by God.

The particulars of how COVID-19 is spliced into such pre-existing conspiracies vary; many claim that the coronavirus epidemic is a mask for quickly moving the rollout of 5G networks, whereas some suggest that 5G experiments in Wuhan, China, have weakened the citizens' immune systems as part of a larger scheme for compulsory vaccination. Most suggest that charts of 5G hot spots suit COVID-19 occurrences or that it has more to do with messing with environmental oxygen (or maybe there's a plot to transform humans into androids that's also in there). Any varieties incorporate all of that, creating a ludicrous myth regarding Microsoft's founder Bill Gates' attempt to depopulate the world utilizing vaccination, 5G and coronavirus.

5G Technology

The first link that started promoting a correlation between 5G as well as the coronavirus outbreak was on a French conspiracy site named Les moutons enrages. A post of January, 2020 floated that the range of millimeter waves used by 5G technologies and Covid-19, the disease triggered by the unique coronavirus, may be linked, referring to reports on Wuhan's installation of towers. 3 months after that in Europe, conspiracists who made identical allegations set mobile poles on fire.

Right-wingers are persuaded that 5G antennas were liable for the influenza pandemic, the systems that build super-fast Web-links. The reasoning is as follows: tiny electromagnetic waves produced from the antennas are forcing our organs to be more susceptible to the infection, or perhaps actually triggering the illness.

The Future of QAnon and Conspiracy Theories

How do we really spread such theories, and how do we avoid them? Take the notion that the leftist Jew billionaire George Soros is, in essence, an immoral con master hell-bent on exploiting the ordinary American interests for his own purposes. Soros has been casted as the Patriarch of Zion in the 21st century. And if you ask other (typically, ultra-far-right) parts of the internet, he's bankrolling everything from Women's March to mass-shooting paid actors to Pizzagate to the Snopes stories debunking certain arguments, with no other explanation than his being leftist, a billionaire, and, of course, Jew.

In 2017, adherents of QAnon more specifically adopted "information warfare" ideas, attempts to mold attitudes and opinions of individuals to manipulate events. Putin's involvement in the 2016 American presidential race was characterized as cyber warfare. In a February 2019 thread named "Welcome to Information Warfare" on QAnon Analysis Site, a poster encouraged fellow members to get ready for a new step in the fight Anons: the quest to win back the [mainstream media] narrative. "Now, QAnon members are attempting to use the same strategies to construct the 2020 political agenda.

The QAnon posts track news and current affairs information on Twitter on dedicated forums on Enchain as well as 8kun. They draw up hashtag lists to hit, produce material and jokes relevant to the democratic events of the day, and exchange tips over how to build popular social networking pages with credible fictional people. The goal, generally speaking, is to overwhelm social media with messages that are pro-Trump, pro-Republican, and non-Democrat or, failing that, simply to hijack and disrupt conversations. Current goals involve Democratic Senate people who opted to impeach the president, especially those who serve districts Trump was carrying in 2016.

7
THE MEDIA AND FAKE NEWS: A WAR HAS BEGAN

Only days into his administration, an enormous overthrow endeavor was propelled against Trump. It got so terrible that, for some time, it truly appeared that Trump would fall flat. Tenacious assaults from the Fake News, Hollywood stars and the Democrats - joined with the conscious damage being completed by Republican Black Hats like John McCain, Paul Ryan, Jeff Flake, Lindsey Graham and others - demoralizingly affected Trump supporters.

An examination of Trump for "Russian agreement" was propelled with ex-FBI boss Robert Mueller named as uncommon investigator. After a long time after night, the CIA's "late night" entertainers derided and disparaged the new president as Trump's endorsement rating dove to as low as 35% in certain surveys.

Counterfeit News, Globalist Democrats and Globalist Republicans, Deep States, European governments, domestics socialists and lease a-crowds of each stripe (paid predominantly by George Soros and Tom Steyer) propelled an overthrow endeavor intended to destabilize Trump and power his acquiescence.

I. QANON DECODED - THE AWAKENING BEGINS

TRUMP DEFIES THE GLOBALISTS

Conquering the savage restriction of the Democrats, some Globalist Republicans, the media and the "universal network," Trump hauled America out of the power devastating TPP (Trans Pacific Partnership and the Paris Climate Accords). He likewise worked together with Russia to defund and annihilate the CIA's "ISIS" fear gathering lastly carry harmony to Syria; and he started the way toward making harmony with North Korea and Russia - activities for which he has been violently assaulted by the Fake News.

Reestablishing coal occupations and deactivating perilous problem areas which the Globalists could use to begin a war whenever were significant achievements.

AND THEN CAME Q-ANON!

Q-Anon is a "Conspiracy Theory" which started with an October 2017 post on the unknown Internet discussion "4-chan," showing up on a sub-gathering titled, "The Storm," made by somebody utilizing the handle Q. The banner who later moved to "8-chan," cases to speak to military knowledge, with access to exceptionally grouped data including the Trump organization and its foes in the universal Cabal.

The various posts, known as "pieces," anticipate, in shockingly exact detail, how the White Hats - tired of seeing a legislature of and claimed by deceivers - are going to steadily destroy a Satanic intrigue of the "Secret government/Black Hats. The scraps blame various liberal Hollywood entertainers, legislators, and high-positioning authorities of taking part in a global kid sex-dealing, kid torment and kid murder ring. As indicated by the hypothesis, Trump orchestrated Robert Mueller to be named not to examine Trump and the Russians, yet rather, to explore Hillary and the Cabal. That is the reason Trump continually alludes to the Mueller test as a "witch chase." The "witch" is Hillary and she is without a doubt being pursued!

The paranoid fear is otherwise called "The Storm" (after Trump's mysterious reference to a coming tempest) and "The Great Awakening."

Trump made it a point to encircle himself with military pioneers and bother the media with talk about a coming "storm." Soon a short time later, Q-Anon started his incredibly prophetic posts."

Q's mysterious posts are various and require long periods of study, explore and deductive rationale to understand. Consider the exact visual cue synopsis set out beneath as a decent "brief training" of what Q has posted. For a progressively exhaustive investigation, research and work through the numerous Q-posts all alone at different destinations that repost them on the web.

- The Cabal never anticipated that Hillary should lose.
- The Cabal didn't know about what the White Hats had coming up for them.
- The Storm is really a military overthrow that selected Trump to lead the political and legitimate parts of what is to be the best "sting" activity.
- Robert Mueller (an ex-marine) really works for the "White Hats" while claiming to restrict Trump.
- The NSA has all the proof need to bring down the Cabal.
- JFK Sr. what's more, JFK Jr. were killed by the Cabal.
- Supreme Court Justice Antonin Scalia was killed by the Cabal.
- The proof should be "cleaned" - that is, gradually presented under the front of different examinations with the goal that it is no longer un-noteworthy proof.
- The overthrow is a moderate movement process - not a "short-term" occasion. Numerous Federal Judges should be selected and FBI and DOJ lawbreakers gradually cleansed and supplanted with loyalists. It is significant not to stun the open at the same time.
- When all is good and well, mass captures of double crossers will be made and a national crisis will be pronounced.
- "Plants, for example, General Mike Flynn and previous Trump battle director Paul Manafort were set under phony examination with the goal that a portion of the NSA proof could be washed and put into play.
- Attorney General Jeff Sessions just professed to be powerless and clumsy. This permitted him to wipe out backstabbers in the FBI and DOJ and lead his own examinations concerning Democrat

I. QANON DECODED - THE AWAKENING BEGINS

voter extortion, the Clinton Foundation, youngster sex dealing and different violations in harmony and calm.
- Hillary and girl Chelsea are into Satanism and black magic.
- Obama's "Iran Deal" was screwy and included gigantic money pay-offs.
- Hillary Clinton and numerous other enormous names are engaged with kid sex dealing, youngster sex torment murder and Satanism.
- Obama is a kid sex stalker.
- The mystery war between the groups stretches out to space.
- The acquiescence's and firings of such a significant number of large men, a considerable lot of them youngster attackers, in media, Hollywood, business and governmental issues is by structure of the White Hats.
- Smaller crooks are being utilized to betray the greater ones.
- The Black Hats have schemed with certain outside "partners" to kill Trump. A few endeavors have been frustrated.
- John McCain faked malignant growth un a bombed endeavor to get away from equity. He was later executed by the military for high treachery with the goal that he was unable to be there to stop Trump's Supreme Court chosen one, Bret Kavanaugh, from being selected.

Hillary and McCain were both spotted wearing lower leg boots for recent months, he for a "ligament injury" and she for a "broken toe" continued while "tumbling down the steps in reverse while drinking espresso." Were they disguising GPS lower leg gadgets? (Your stick is on an inappropriate side, Senator.) McCain was later found changing his boot from option to left, and clarified it away by saying his other leg was getting worn out!!!

•Trump has gone through about two years stacking the government legal executive with loyalists ahead of time of preliminaries.

•The official accounts of World War I and II are bogus.

•Tech front men, for example, Mark Zuckerberg and Elon Musk are CIA.

•Ed Snowden was pursued by NSA, yet is presently helping out the White Hats.

- The state administration of California has begun out of control fires so as to get progressively government cash.

- Other Black Hat Republicans had to leave (Jeff Flake, Paul Ryan, Bob Corker and so forth).

- Over 50,000 fixed arraignments - huge numbers of them enormous names - will in the end be unlocked.

- Cabal lawbreakers will be attempted by military courts be sent to the U. S's. Guantanamo jail in Cuba.

- The first-class DC-based "Pizzagate" kid sex and torment murder ring is genuine and will be uncovered.

- Guantanamo Bay military jail will be topped off with Cabal individuals and their operators.

- The powerful Rothschilds and George Soros will fall.

- During "The Storm," Trump will utilize crisis PDA alarms to sidestep the media and convey straightforwardly to the American individuals.

- The Democrat Party is being set up for Trump to obliterate it.

- Blacks will forsake the Democrat Party when they learn of Hillary's hijacking and sex-dealing of Haitian youngsters.

- Other world pioneers (Putin, Xi) are working with Trump to crush the Globalists for the last time.

- The Republicans would be cleansed of hostile to Trump backstabbers, and afterward roll onto a fruitful 2018 mid-term decisions.

- The truth about the 9/11 assaults will be uncovered in due time.

- The Israel-Palestine issue will be settled calmly for the last time. There will be not any more Israeli hostility or extension.

Adding assurance to the Q-Anon wonder are the horrible predominant press assaults focused on Q, just as the undeniable certainty that Trump himself, on MANY events, both by tweets and face to face, has purposely furnished Q-devotees with clear indications that he thinks about Q. Is Q-Anon without a doubt? Indeed, it is looking increasingly more as though

Trump is honored and sponsored up by some imperceptible power that is incredible - is it not? The coming months will tell. Meanwhile, remember this introduction, and spread it generally.

THE PEDO-MONSTER ART OF ALEX PODESTA

Numerous individuals currently think about the suspected pedo-beast Podesta Brothers, John and Tony. John was Hillary's crusade administrator, and Tony (current whereabouts obscure, presumably nabbed) was one of the most persuasive lobbyists in DC until Robert Mueller (who is working with Trump) put him bankrupt in late 2017. Here are a couple of bits of poop created by "craftsmen" that Tony Podesta, by his own affirmation, positioned among his top choices!

Torment and murder of kids - Evidently, that is the thing that "Alice in Wonderland" (Hillary's codename as indicated by E-sends hacked by NSA) intends to pedo-beasts.

OK show such photographs in your home? Or then again arrange a gathering for the "craftsman?" Podesta did!

Trump's best three Globalist Republican adversaries in the Senate (Flake, McCain and Corker) are gone, and the fourth (Graham) is presently his woofing pet pooch.

1 and 2. Q Anon adherents are developing in number so quick that the Fake News has propelled numerous assaults on the development. /3. Late night anchor person Bill Maher, got out as a pedo-beast by Q-Anon, did an extensive fragment taunting the "Conspiracy Theory."

General Mike Flynn

8
HOW THE PATRIOTS FIGHT THE ENEMY?

QAnon consists of like-minded individuals that don't agree on everything but share some common beliefs. We believe the President is working hard to Make America Great Again and his enemies have been conspiring against him since the day he was elected. If you watch the news or read a newspaper, there's so many negative stories and it's dividing our country. We want to educate and unite the people.

As a veteran, I'd like to thank everyone who has served our country at any point of this nation's history. Maybe the military isn't for you and that's perfectly acceptable, there are many ways to be a Patriot. In any war, there are soldiers on the front lines and their soldiers working to support the people fighting on the front lines. If you believe in the cause and you're determined to Make America Great Again, then QAnon is the best place for you to join regardless of the role you select for yourself. QAnon relies on good people to stand up to the global power elites and we don't care if you want to be the quarterback, the shooting guard or a goalie. Join the team and get in where you fit in.

Feeding the Front Lines

If you're hard core, you might consider becoming a baker. A baker is someone that cooks the breadcrumbs and creates Q drop interpretations for the movement. The research can be long and demanding due to the

I. QANON DECODED - THE AWAKENING BEGINS

sheer volume of information being disseminated. Bakers carefully dissect each drop to scan for connections to current events or posts which may shed light on the true message being revealed by Q. The bakers take the crumbs and create "bread" and/or "dough" to feed the patriots in the movement. It's quite complex so Q provided this warning, "These are crumbs and you cannot imagine the full and complete picture." The bread created by bakers is a valuable resource for teaching others the wisdom found with the drops and the bakers are essential to progressing our knowledge and understanding of what is really happening in the world today.

Moments of reflection can be the key to better understanding. Whether you create your own timeline or follow the interpretations of others, stay vigilant and informed. Bakers are necessary to supply starving minds with much needed informational nutrition because the MSM is so determined on delivering negative stories and fake news.

We're all busy with personal and professional lives that limit the amount of time we can devote to even the worthiest causes. A new baby on the way, a sick relative or a promotion at work are all legitimate reasons for not being able to dedicate the time and energy needed to be a baker. However, that doesn't mean that you can't contribute in other ways.

Local rallies are an excellent way to join like-minded individuals and create the organization necessary for our movement to advance. POTUS Trump uses these rallies to speak directly to us without interference from the MSM. Also, he uses these interactions to show subtle signs of acknowledgment and appreciation. If you look carefully, POTUS Trump can be seen making "Air Q's" where he uses his finger to draw the letter Q in the air. Vice President Pence has also tweeted a photo of himself next a police officer with the QAnon patch.

Finally, you can send financial support to members of the movement who have demonstrated their commitment to overthrowing the Deep State and taking back our country. Be careful with who you choose to support and make sure they're involved in the movement for the right reasons. Now that QAnon has become so popular, people with low morals are trying to jump on the bandwagon. They are easy spot and thanks to the internet you can follow the breadcrumbs back to beginning of their involvement. It's possible to have a dramatic change of heart after witnessing all of the research completed by the QAnon community but someone who fronted an HRC field office in Boston, MA is probably not playing for the same team as you are.

As Q supporters, we are bringing a systemic process of reasoning to our participation in the war of Good vs Evil. I feel it is my duty and obligation to fight any enemy both foreign and domestic who would attempt to destroy this great nation. You might have heard that QAnon is some sort of Live Action Role Play (LARP) experience but there's way too much evidence that the movement is real. We, The People are awake and that's what they fear most. If you look, you can't help but see and, in my eyes, you're all patriots.

9
THE OLD DEEP STATE PUPPETS

President Eisenhower cautioned us. He called the "Underground government" at work the "military-mechanical complex." There will consistently be individuals in a general public who are more willing than others, increasingly inclined to harassing, taking, and making asses out of themselves.

In eighteenth century, political rationalist William Godwin watched, if an administration has any real reason whatsoever, is to shield these individuals from doing mischief to their kindred people. Yet, after some time, these domineering jerks will swarm government and other ventures. At that point, rather than monitoring these bugs, government game them power, in any event, financing a sort of phony decency. Their predations, figments, and vanities became open arrangement.

Every significant industry – media, training, human services and money – draw in these domineering jerks and asses. Yet, the Deep State treats as kind of a fertilizer heap to a group of pigs. Before long, they will establish and floundering in the greatest load of abused assets in the entire history.

Today, the Deep State's specialists tell you to remove your belt and shoes at air terminals. Attempt to dive a lake in your patio, or let your adolescent child chip away at the family homestead, and they will put forth a defense of it. They sneak and spy searching for insider facts they can endeavor to pay off you. They charge. They control. Furthermore, they control.

In any case, the ones that are crazy are simply the plot individuals and this must be halted right away.

This shadowy mystery government whose extreme objective is the usage of the purported New World Order, is calling the shots on the world's manikin heads of state and commanders of industry. The term Deep State has as of late picked up footing, notwithstanding the utilization of terms like; shadow government, plot, Rothschild Kazazian Mafia, The Powers That Be, the Luciferians, Illuminati, Elite; all referencing a similar gathering of covered up Luciferian Satanists that loathe and burglarize individuals. - The Deep State is a selected insider-government inside in the administration. They are not inspired by governmental issues, just in cash and power, and will keep doing what they are doing, until they can't do it any longer.

How, the secret government works

An intricate snare of spinning entryways between government, the military-modern complex, Wall Street, and Silicon Valley solidifies the premiums of protection temporary workers, banisters, military crusades, and both outside and household observation insight, the media, and social insurance, just to give some examples.

Cash, the economy, and government have all changed since the breakdown of the Bretton Woods understanding and the finish of gold-sponsored cash. When on August 15, 1971, President Nixon pounded the last nail in the casket of legitimate cash by abrogating gold sponsorship for the US-Dollar, the world's save money.

This was not by any means the only purpose behind the significant changes that followed. There was additionally the acquaintance of Communist China with private enterprise, the fall of the Soviet Union, and the ascent of the Internet, to give some examples.

After the disintegration of the Soviet in 1991, the DS confronted the greatest danger to its reality It not, at this point had a conceivable foe. From that point forward, it has put U.S. jackboots on the ground in a takedown of a progression of pseudo-adversaries – all ludicrously mediocre.

I. QANON DECODED - THE AWAKENING BEGINS

It is war, not harmony that pays

The individuals who do the reasoning and the plotting, then again, have another plan. They are similarly as content with an annihilation as a triumph. - Victory, and the harmony that followed World War II, nearly put them bankrupt. It is war, not harmony that pays. Furthermore, war pays well, also all the individual freedoms that are appropriated with each manufactured war.

The Trillion Dollar Industry

The U.S. "security" industry has about $1 trillion every year in spending power. You can purchase a great deal of votes with that sort of cash. The Deep State stays in control. The fix is consistently in.

The covert government covers up on display and goes a long way past the military-modern complex. While most residents are in any event inactively mindful of the reconnaissance state and the trick between the legislature and the corporate heads of Wall Street, scarcely any individuals know about how much the knowledge elements of the administration have been redistributed to privatized bunches that are not dependent upon oversight or responsibility by people in general.

The Money Suckers

Additionally, while Wall Street and the government drain cash out of the economy, consigning countless individuals to neediness and detaining a bigger number of individuals than China - an authoritarian state with four times a greater number of individuals than the US. The underground government has, since 9/11, fabricated what might be compared to three Pentagons, an enlarged state mechanical assembly that keeps barrier temporary workers, insight contractual workers, and has financed privatized non-responsible NGOs.

Large Business, called Corpocracy helps the underground government. The spinning entryway among government and Wall Street cash permits top firms to extend to premium employment opportunities to senior government authorities and military yes-men. Money Street is a definitive establishment for the secret government in light of the fact that the unbelievable measure of cash it creates can give these comfortable occupations to those in government after they resign. Nepotism rules as the rotating entryway between Wall Street and the government encourage a lot of residential difficulty

"Bank bailouts, tax cuts, and protection from enactment that would control Wall Street, political givers, and lobbyists. The senior government authorities, ex-commanders, and elevated level insight agents who take an interest wind up with multi-million-dollar homes in which they spend their retirement years, padded by a clean heap of speculations."

How did The Deep State appear?

Despite the fact that the Deep State is a well-established arranged substance, initially it might have been named in an unexpected way. Insiders are of the sentiment that eventually it is the posterity of the military-mechanical complex, while others state it appeared with the Federal Reserve Act in 1913, when Woodrow Wilson commented;

"We have come to be one of the most exceedingly awful managed, one of the most totally controlled and ruled governments in the cultivated world, not, at this point a legislature by conviction and the vote of the lion's share, however an administration by the sentiment and coercion of a little gathering of prevailing men."

This semi mystery plot is calling the shots in Washington, and a significant part of the world is kept up under the weight of a corporatist belief system that blossoms with deregulation, redistributing, deindustrialization, and financialization, yielding interminable war and monetary dominion abroad, while uniting the interests of the government.

The Deep State is an administration inside a legislature that works off expense dollars however isn't compelled by the constitution, nor are its plots wrecked by political movements. In this world - where the secret government capacities without any potential repercussions - it doesn't make a difference who is president inasmuch as the person propagates the war on fear, which serves this interconnected snare of corporate uncommon interests and insincere geopolitical goals.

"For whatever length of time that allotment bills get sat back, advancement records get affirmed, dark (i.e., mystery) financial plans get elastic stepped, extraordinary assessment sponsorships for specific companies are endorsed without contention, as long as an excessive number of clumsy inquiries are not posed, the riggings of the half breed state will work quietly".

Is there trust later on?

Without a doubt there is trust, and the epilog is fast approaching. At present, strife and agitation keep on building. Be that as it may, different gatherings, foundations, associations, and segments of the people from all edges of the political range, including Silicon Valley, Occupy, the Tea Party, Anonymous, WikiLeaks, revolutionaries, libertarians from both the left and right, Whistleblowers like Edward Snowden and others are starting to energetically address and reject the maze of intensity employed by the underground government.

Will these gatherings - can we, the individuals - beat the separation and vanquish strategies used to subdue contradict? That relies upon what number of us wake up and join in the significance of manufacturing a future with opportunity and flourishing. It lies in our own hands, while help is on its way, as long as we as a whole get and stay positive and roused to destroy this Deep State Mafia, once and for eternity! Think about this; Our Creator has made planet Earth and its kin, not to be decimated by a little gathering of Mafiosi, called the Deep State!

10
THE NEW DEEP STATE PUPPETS

OPERATION MOCKINGBIRD

Prior to proceeding, I need to make it clear that, albeit a portion of the activities, tasks and individuals inside the purported three-letter offices may be inferred or legitimately got out as 'terrible entertainers' of the most noticeably awful kind, it is my and our firm conviction that by far most of individuals from these offices are acceptable, well behaved individuals who are regularly placing their own lives at risk to guarantee the wellbeing of residents. Q himself affirmed this more than once too, so it is significant that, in proceeding, we comprehend that this entire debilitated net was woven by just a couple in charge, some who were more willing than others, some most likely reluctantly came into it by methods for immense totals of cash and others even by methods for coercion. It is intelligent to likewise acknowledge that most were just after requests. At long last, most individuals from these offices were rarely included, inferred or, I accept, even mindful of the devilish web by any means.

Doing a direct hunt of Operation Mockingbird promptly featured a few disparities. It was striking how a few outcomes would be characterized as 'affirmed' or 'in principle', while simultaneously there were others with clear proof that the presence of this activity was a reality and even formally reported. It unfolded upon me this was precisely the same dissat-

I. QANON DECODED- THE AWAKENING BEGINS

isfaction I encountered when investigating the 9/11 occurrence; the battle to control oneself between the substantiates realities, the concealment, the hypotheses and the plain lies concealing the shrouded motivation. This time was extraordinary, however: 1) Q, who, for the time being, I accepted, approached the genuine intel, makes reference to it as a reality that should have been investigated; and 2) The query items highlighted very much recorded realities about the presence of this activity, including the transcripts of an official Congress examination concerning the charges of such an activity.

Everything considered, I currently understand that subliminally another significant seed was planted: I would be starting here on never at any point see something being made light of as a paranoid notion the equivalent again — never. This would later become what we called 'the red pill' impact, taken from the film The Matrix. This was just the seed, however; the genuine red pill itself and its impact would just come a lot later.

Activity Mockingbird was a mystery crusade by the United States Central Intelligence Agency (CIA) to impact media. Started during the 1950s, it was at first sorted out by Cord Meyer and Allen W Dulles, and it was later driven by Frank Wisner when Dulles turned into the leader of the CIA. The association selected driving American columnists into a system, to help present the CIA's perspectives, and supported some understudy and social associations and magazines as fronts. As it created, it additionally attempted to impact outside media and political battles, notwithstanding exercises by other working units of the CIA. A portion of the data I discovered online attempted to minimize this activity to fundamentally constraining it to the CIA getting data by the tapping of two columnists' telephones. Looking past this make light of the realities into further authority records, transcripts of authentic examinations and numerous truthful articles expounded on it throughout the years, made it extremely evident that there was much more to this than just the tapping of two telephones. Discovering a few words from a discourse by JFK, I likewise really wanted to think about whether he was not really alluding to the unfortunate authority over the media that he was clearly mindful of when he stated: "Its arrangements are disguised, not distributed. Its mix-ups are covered, not featured. Its nonconformists are hushed, not applauded. No use is addressed, no gossip is printed and no mystery is uncovered." I additionally found another comment that JFK made in regards to the CIA itself, in any case, investigating it, some said he never said it openly. Nonetheless, what seems to be accepted is that President Kennedy, as the monstrosity of the Bay of Pigs (a bombed military intrusion of Cuba embraced by the CIA) calamity got back home to him, said to perhaps the most elevated authority of his organization that he 'needed to fragment the CIA in a thousand pieces and disperse it to the breezes'.

My undeniable concern was that all that I found so far was alluding to numerous years prior, yet Q referenced it as though it was as of now despite everything assuming a significant job. That was until I discovered another statement from 1981, at the same time, before connecting any an incentive to it, I realized I needed to by one way or another attempt to confirm it, which I in the long run did. On 21 September 2014, at 8:59pm, Barbara Honegger wrote in an email: "Genuinely I for one was the Source for that William Casey quote. He said it at an early February 1981 gathering in the Roosevelt Room in the West Wing of the White House which I joined in, and I quickly told my dear companion and political back up parent Senior White House Correspondent Sarah McClendon, who at that point opened up to the world about it without naming the source." The statement was plain and no doubt alluding to Operation Mockingbird. CIA Director William Casey said at the referenced gathering: "We'll realize our disinformation program is finished when everything the American open accepts is bogus." Agreed, they may have balanced the tasks or even the name of the activity at this point, however on a basic level that reality stays; certain individuals inside the CIA were resolved, for whatever clouded explanation, to control the media in totality and with that likewise control what residents are being told and in the long run what the majority will accept to be reality. This activity was not constrained to the U.S. just, yet in addition spread out to the remainder of the world. For the time being, the goals, plans and reliability of the CIA as one of the three-letter offices Q referenced were obviously sketchy without a doubt. This made me wonder, however; what different activities like this one were recorded?

OPERATION PAPERCLIP

Investigating some different activities, it was very hard to choose which ones to look into, as the length of the rundown was bewildering. It additionally relies upon what you would enter in the pursuit field; 'division of barrier mystery tasks' would concoct its own rundown while changing DOD to CIA or FBI would think of others. Including 'connivance' or 'claimed' to the pursuit would some of the time twofold the outcomes. Three of the outcomes that truly got my attention, each for its own reasons, were Operation Paperclip, which included the Nazi researchers after WW2, Operation Midnight Climax, which appears to have included LSD testing, and Project Muttra, which didn't bode well at all until further notice and therefore fascinated me.

Activity Paperclip is really referenced on the official CIA site, yet from the start I saw it being 'accused' on the race after WW2 between the U.S. what's more, Russia to 'seize whatever number German researchers as could be expected under the circumstances fully expecting the Cold War'. Because of this, just as the way that I currently had motivation to address elective thought processes of the three-letter organizations, particularly the CIA, I focused on different assets as opposed to their own site. It was acceptable to know, however, that they clearly acknowledged this particular activity as genuine.

In an undercover issue initially named Operation Overcast, however later named Operation Paperclip, about 1.6k of German researchers (alongside their families) were transferred to the US. From the start, the activity in my psyche could be advocated, in spite of the fact that simultaneously I asked why these individuals would then not be pursued for atrocities. All things considered, from all the post-war inhumanities we have educated of through history, the hair-raising trials that were done, particularly on youngsters, despite everything frequented some today. Indeed, at that point I discovered this: in spite of the fact that he authoritatively endorsed the activity, President H. Truman disallowed the organization from enrolling any Nazi individuals or dynamic Nazi supporters. In any case, authorities inside the JIOA (Joint Intelligence Objectives Agency) and (OSS), the harbinger to CIA, avoided this mandate by dispensing with or whitewashing implicating proof of conceivable atrocities from the researchers' records, defending their activities by saying their knowledge was essential to the nation's post-war endeavors. However, I took a gander at this, or attempting to comprehend their avocation, the reality remained that they gruffly overlooked the authority of the president.

Another disturbing reality ended up being explicit positions these individuals were set in. Another most notable volunteers were Werner von Braun, a specialized executive at the PARC in Germany who was used in building up the deadly V2 rocket that crushed England. Von Braun and others were brought to Texas and New Mexico as 'war office unique workers' to help the US Army with Missiles. Von later became the executive of NASA's MSFC and the main designer of the Saturn V dispatch vehicle. It shows up as though a portion of the subtleties of the activities were released and tension built to a point where a few of the Paperclip researchers were later examined because of their connections with the Nazi Party during the war. In any case, at long last, just a single Paperclip researcher (Georg Rickhey) was officially gone after for any wrongdoing and no Paperclip researcher was seen as liable of any wrongdoing, in America or Germany. In 1947, Georg Rickhey, who went to the United States under Operation Paperclip in 1946, was come back to Germany to stand preliminary at the Dora Trial, where he was vindicated. Others may have also been explored, yet the U.S. insight specialists were so spellbound by their strategic they went to uncommon lengths to shield their enlisted people from criminal examiners at the U.S. Branch of Justice. One of the more abominable cases was that of Nazi avionics analyst Emil Salmon, who, during the war, had helped burned down a gathering place loaded up with Jewish ladies and kids. Salmon was protected by U.S. authorities at Wright Air Force Base in Ohio subsequent to being sentenced for wrongdoings by a 'denazification' court in Germany.

Nazis were by all account not the only researchers searched out by U.S. insight specialists after the finish of World War II. In Japan, the U.S. Armed force put on its finance Dr Shiro Ishii, the leader of the Japanese Imperial Army's profile fighting unit. Dr Ishii had conveyed a wide scope of natural and compound operators against Chinese and Allied soldiers, and had likewise worked an enormous research community in Manchuria, where he directed bio weapons investigates Chinese, Russian and American detainees of war. Ishii tainted detainees with lockjaw, gave them typhoid-bound tomatoes, created plague-contaminated insects, contaminated ladies with syphilis and detonated germ bombs more than many POWs. Among different monstrosities, Ishii's records show that he frequently performed 'dissections' on live casualties. In an arrangement brought forth by General Douglas MacArthur, Ishii turned over in excess of 10,000 pages of his 'inquire about discoveries' to the U.S. Armed force, stayed away from arraignment for atrocities and was welcome to address at Ft. Detrick, the U.S. Armed force bio weapons investigate focus close to Frederick, Maryland.

The huge rundown of enterprises that these individuals were put in was awe-inspiring: flying and rocketry, engineering and hardware (counting direction frameworks, radar and satellites), material science, physical science and medication, (counting natural weapons, compound weapons and space medication).

II

WHAT IS A CONSPIRACY THEORY?

The phrase comes from two separate words. The first, "conspiracy," is defined by the modern Webster's Dictionary as, "The Act of conspiring together." That's not terribly helpful, but the much older famous 1828 edition written by Noah Webster himself is. A mix of men for an abhorrent reason; an understanding between at least two people, to carry out some wrongdoing in show; especially, a blend to submit injustice, or energize subversion or rebellion against the legislature of an express; a plot; as a trick against the life of a ruler; a connivance against the administration. Suddenly, we get into something much juicier: crime, treason, sedition, insurrection often aimed at something in government. Interesting. To this day, this is what the majority of conspiracy theories are actually aimed at, yet Webster wrote this 200 years ago!

We will see a greater amount of this in a later part, however Webster really includes as his solitary verification, a connivance that forty Jews had plotted against the Apostle Paul to execute him. They went to the central clerics and older folks and stated, 'We have carefully bound ourselves by a pledge to taste no food till we have murdered Paul. Presently subsequently you, alongside the committee, pull out to the tribune to bring him down to you, just as you would decide his case all the more precisely. Furthermore, we are prepared to murder him before he draws close'" (Acts 23:12-15). It was an alternate America when a proof for a mainstream definition

I. QANON DECODED - THE AWAKENING BEGINS

originated from the Bible. These Jews were the strict pioneers, profoundly in bed with the political elites of their day, so the content accommodates his definition. Plainly, intrigues of significant level legislative issues have been with us for a long, long time.

His subsequent definition is likewise worth perusing. "In law, an understanding between at least two people, erroneously and noxiously to prosecute, or get to be arraigned, an honest individual of crime." Notice this isn't generous in inspiration. It is malignant. It follows blameless individuals to ensure the liable. Along these lines, apparently what this first expression of the expression brings to our understanding is that insidious individuals do malignant, dissident, criminal, and even treasonous things, things they plan covertly which nobody thinks about however themselves.

How about we go to "hypothesis." This is a fascinating word. This time, I will start with the 1828 definition. Webster calls it, "Hypothesis, a regulation or plan of things, which ends in theory or thought." He includes this is "here taken in an ominous sense." Meanwhile, the main definition given by the current Webster's is, "A conceivable or logically satisfactory general rule or assortment of standards offered to clarify marvels."

So here we have a negative and a positive definition for a hypothesis. One methods hypothesis; the other basically manages science (to be reasonable, the 1828 has as the subsequent definition, "A work of the general standards of any science; as the hypothesis of music"). What I am seeing here is a potential distinction in how individuals can see the expression "paranoid fear." Some view it as a logically situated examination concerning open realities that don't exactly include, maybe something like the manner in which Sherlock Holmes consistently approached explaining a case.

Notwithstanding, given what we saw with the CIA's secret activity to truly change the expression and make it something individuals won't have any desire to take part in, it appears that they needed individuals to consider it as indicated by an untethered, wild and insane hypothesis, grounded in only the likes and minds of insane individuals making the hypothesis. This is absolutely what number of individuals characterize the expression today and it is very disturbing, in fact.

MR. BABYLON

At the point when individuals utilize the expression "paranoid notion" today, it is to be an idea plug and a contention executioner. All you need to do nowadays to ensure nobody addresses what you are stating is to mark the individuals who differ as trick scholars. Game over. Like a man-made weaponized infection, its sole design is to taint an individual's mind and devastate all endeavors it may make to scrutinize an official story. More regrettable, as one companion disclosed to me just today, it is utilized in a belittling way, frequently went with ridiculing, scornful remarks. It is mock, not reason.

That may not be the spoken or even comprehended plan of everybody utilizing the term. All things considered, it ought to be without question this is the thing that the term in truth is utilized for a significant part of the time. In the event that you toss out "fear inspired notion" towards an individual or thought that they are engaging, you are adequately disclosing to them that they are insane, nut-jobs, wackos, or more terrible, foes of state or the republic itself. That is actually how the CIA and Bush discussed the expression. What's more, it is has worked itself out to flawlessness in the regular speech and comprehension of its significance. This is an enormous move from the manner in which the expression and the thought behind it was utilized in ancient times.

A NEW PHENOMENON?

A LOT OF PEOPLE THINK THAT paranoid notions are another wonder. This is definitely not the case. For if that were valid, it would imply that there have been no connivances in mankind's history. How might I say this? Since, where there are no connivances, there is nothing genuine that makes individuals question an official account. Best case scenario, the uncertainty originates from their own wild creative mind. Most things in life are not connivances. Most things in life are likewise not addressed. In all actuality, most things in life are additionally generally irrelevant as well. Be that as it may, in a connivance, any scheme, there are consistently openings in the story. Those gaps are what makes questions emerge. Those inquiries at that point lead to questions and questions lead to paranoid ideas. However, numerous occasions in history have driven individuals to question an official story. In a portion of those, we realize that not all things happen as the partisan loyalty told the individuals.

I. QANON DECODED - THE AWAKENING BEGINS

Truth be told, in a portion of those, genuine connivances were occurring. In this part, I need to give a short history of a specific type of fear inspired notion known as the bogus banner. A significant part of the material for this part has been winnowed from various talks given by Richard Dolan, who has accomplished some gigantic work on this history of paranoid fears. My work is obliged to him.

WHAT IS A FALSE FLAG?

In the first place, I ought to ask, what is a bogus banner? The term originates from the universe of pilfering on the high oceans. Ahoy, Matey! (Did you realize you can make an interpretation of the past sentence into "Privateer" utilizing Google: "Th' term originates from th' world o' piratin' on th' high oceans." But I diverge). This is the universe of Captain Jack Sparrow and the Black Pearl. In any case, this is no Disney film or amusement park ride!

A privateer would cruise his boat close to a foe vessel with the adversary's banner or an unbiased banner raised high up his own, in this way tricking them into deduction he was neighborly. At that point, out of nowhere, he would raise the skull and crossbones and assault. For what reason would he do that? In the first place, since privateers truly had a code of respect, not at all like the individuals who pull off the present bogus banner occasions! Second, the banner itself would alarm the resistance.

Just when a cannonball was going to tear through his own lodge would poorly people, clueless commander understand that it was actually a privateer who was gazing at him over his bow.

We discover the language of "bogus banner" being utilized as ahead of schedule as the 1680s. One epic of the period lets us know,

Yet, they had barely moved sails what way, when they were found by the three galleys and a warship, having a place with the island, which having beguiled them with a *bogus banner*, assaulted them so surprisingly, that the Egyptian commander, being not able to guard himself against so extraordinary a power, was obliged to yield up himself, his slaves, boat what not. [spelling modernized, italics mine]

MR. BABYLON

The Elements of International Law of 1863 gives us a past filled with how bogus banners on the high oceans were getting so normal, among privateers as well as among countries heading out to fight, that worldwide law must be made to moderate the issue.

By the 42d article of the arrangement of the 30th of April, 1725, among Spain and Austria, it was concurred that whoever took letters of marque and retaliation from any legislature not his own ought to be treated as a privateer, and by the fifth article of the settlement finished up with the Netherlands in 1714, and by the fourteenth article of the commended bargain of 1795 with the United States, it was concurred that whoever took commissions or letters of marque from another State, which was at war with both of the contracting parties, ought to be considered in a similar character of privateers ... The privateer law of Spain of 1801 ... builds up that each vessel will be considered as a privateer which raises a bogus banner, or raises no banner, or battles under another banner than its actual one.

Disrupting these guidelines was considered "very serious." Thus, we find at the episode of WWI,

An observer had stated that he saw that the assaulting German boats which besieged [Scarborough] had raised the British ensign. [This] would, whenever checked, be a grave break of worldwide law if the British ensign remained lifted after the assault had started. Adrift, as ashore, the utilization of bogus hues in war is forbidden.

The language of bogus banners has in progressively current occasions come to be utilized of intentionally arranged assaults accused on one gathering when in truth they were executed by another person. At their heart, bogus banners are a type of purposeful publicity. Be that as it may, they move amazing to activities, activities which regularly have a lethal result for certain individuals.

They are normally done with the goal that other preplanned results, anything from changing general conclusion on an issue (assessment that could never show signs of change were they not seeing the bogus banner unfurl before their eyes), to passing tyrant laws, or supporting military attacks, or proclaiming some in any case hard to difficult to-offer to-the

I. QANON DECODED - THE AWAKENING BEGINS

open result. The relations to paranoid notions are anything but difficult to see when you understand that things like mass acts of mass violence, the fall of the twin towers, or the arrival of fatal maladies into a populace are called both fears inspired notions and bogus banners.

12
WHAT IS THE INFORMATION WAR?

First and foremost, let us tackle the definition and facets of the information war. Information war or information warfare is an evolving area of interest for policymakers and defense planners. Our growing accessibility to information has brought a massive revolution to military strategy. In particular, the U.S. military perceives information as a valuable warfare method because of its ability to influence national power. Information warfare is deeply rooted in our culture's dependency on cyberspace, the internet, computers, and other forms of technology for communication.

According to Dan Kuehl of the National Defense University, information warfare can be defined as the conflict between two states utilizing the information landscape. Another way to look at information warfare is the manipulation of information that is accepted and trusted by a target without their awareness. In this way, the target is convinced to make decisions in the interest of the individual or group carrying out information warfare.

In far simpler terms, one can consider it a type of hacking because it largely concerns operations that exploit information resources. However, "hacking" downplays the true danger and severity of information war. If you think about it, the free flow of information via the internet or other technological means is key to how many nations conduct business, social, and international relations. To use information warfare means to destabilize a nation or a society on several fronts.

Information warfare can be carried out in a variety of ways. First, information warfare is used to attack and disrupt communications carried out over electromagnetic transmissions. This refers to jamming and electronic countermeasures that can be used to weaken or neutralize military operations, communications, and weapon guidance systems. Jamming can also be applied to civil circumstances, like air traffic control systems or the European Trail Traffic Management System (ERTMS), which can provide full control over trains. In civil or military situations, electronic jamming is sure to cause confusion and chaos.

The second form of information warfare, and probably the most familiar to us, is cyber-attacks. This refers to attacks that are launched against digital networks via the internet. This form of information warfare is usually extremely costly to businesses and financial structures. For example, Sony Pictures and Talk-Talk has experienced massive damage in terms of reputation and cost after a cyberattack. Moreover, cyberattacks can mount enormous damage on industrial systems and infrastructure, such as manufacturing plants, power plants, and water and gas utilities.

All that being said, it is important to think of information warfare as a multifaceted concept that seems to grow more complex as technology grows. Remember, war is no long just waged on a traditional battlefield. Enemy attacks are cutting across space, time, cyberspace, and more. We have to look at information as both a resource and as a weapon that can perform across multiple domains.

WHY IS THE INFORMATION WAR NECESSARY?

If you look back on history, you will see that technological advancements were at the forefront of a number of major revolutions. The cannon transformed warfare in the 15th century. The machine and industrial era transformed the World Wars. In our current era of information and electronic communication, digitization is fundamentally changing war and is becoming a necessity to any country's modernization and combat readiness. The information war has already broken out.

It has become a necessity because as communication technology evolves and grows, the ways in which those systems can be exploited also grow. If a country lacks the right command structure to control information technology, there could be unprecedented threats to civilian infrastructure. This is why it is very important to understand how all these things work. As such, it is also very important to understand how information technology can affect a country's modernization, diplomacy, military capabilities, and more. That being said, let's take a look at why information technology is a necessity.

First and foremost, success in information warfare defines success in combat and firepower superiority. Information warfare has the ability to also achieve more victories at a smaller cost. So, how exactly does information warfare achieve this? It begins with understanding that weapons and information are in the hands of the people. If you boil it down, people are the at the core of combat power because of how they can control the flow of information.

So, if you take the flow of information and integrate it into manpower, materials, and capacity, you can ultimately control victory or defeat in warfare. Moreover, information technology can ensure capacity efficiency, which is key to be a strong combat power. If you have military capacity, but do not use it well, you can cause unnecessary waste and damage, which is not fruitful. Utilizing information warfare technology can easily solve this problem and ensure that a country's military construction is of a higher standard. So, we should definitely take the necessary steps.

Secondly, information warfare technology is necessary because it greatly improves a country's weapons system, equipment and more. Investing in information technology, networks, and weapons system is valuable for any military trying to transition to information warfare. Some key technologies include remote-sensing technology, communications technology, precision-guided weapons systems, electric warfare weapons systems, and any other guidance systems, control systems, and intelligence systems. These systems are very handy and useful.

Improving these systems with information technology also means improving reconnaissance. This way countries and their respective military can obtain vital information in a timely manner and gain better clarity and understanding about their enemies, which is very crucial. Moreover, information technology can improve strategies for air defense systems and help countries detect enemy movements early on. So, a country with the right information warfare technology get stay up to date and stay prepared for any unwanted situations.

While information technology can improve defense mechanisms, it can also be used to strengthen offensive mechanisms, which is great. Some of these mechanisms include tactical guided missile attack systems, landing operations, electronic weapons systems, and minelaying systems. With the help of information technology, these systems will allow countries to have a high-precision attack capabilities and stronger chances of surviving attacks.

Lastly, information technology streamlines strategic communications. Information technology essentially brings all the different domains of the military into a single, cohesive network. This ensures that information can be gained in real time in every domain, which is very convenient. This also ensures that there is coordination in the vertical and horizontal chains of warfare command for the sake of efficiently finding the best solution.

Information war and information technology is a necessity because the battlefields are changing. We need to change too. Our systems need to improve. In our current era, potential adversaries are presenting challenges that exist far away from the traditional line of combat. They are constantly engaging in information warfare that has clear impacts on the United States. The only way to counter these attacks is to adjust their strategies and diligently work on operations that match the level and type of threat used by adversaries.

STATEMENT OF THE PENTAGON

The pervasiveness of information warfare is not lost on the Pentagon. As a matter of fact, the Pentagon has been stepping up their game in the world of digital warfare. Recently, in 2018, the Army carried out the first electronic attack since the Cold War during Saber Strike. It is an annual joint exercise that occurs throughout Estonia, Poland, Lithuania, and Latvia and aims to prepare individuals to efficiently respond to regional crises and security needs. During the exercise they used a new tool that was invented by the Rapid Capabilities Office or RCO, who has been responsible for the development of electronic warfare prototypes.

Meanwhile, the Navy has invested a $100 million award to Advanced Technology International to accelerate the development of information warfare tools and prototypes. The goal is to have a wealth of information war tools operational as soon as possible. Additionally, Navy leaders highlighted the necessity of information warfare at the 2018 Sea-Air-Exposition to ensure they are cultivating a more aware community.

Lastly, the Army and the Joint Information operations Warfare Center have also joined in the pursuit of growing information technology. The Army and the JIOWC, who is responsible for integrating the information operations of the Department of Defense under a single command, dedicated an entire day to researching new information war technology. They primarily focused on how to efficiently combine physical and information operations and how to utilize information to get a psychological response.

These different activities are vital parts of the Pentagon's new approach to information warfare. Until recently, military leaders have been shelving electronic warfare tactics while they focused on the wars in Iraq and Afghanistan. In these countries, they did not need to worry about electronic warfare because the airwaves, at the time, were relatively easy to sift through. However, in recent years, more technically skilled adversaries have been appearing in other areas like Eastern Europe and South Pacific.

In particular, Russia has made themselves a formidable adversary due to their considerable use of hybrid, electronic warfare tactics in Syria and Ukraine. They have also recently revealed that they are establishing an entirely new branch dedicated to developing information warfare tools. Another country that has staked their claim in the world of information warfare is China. China has been testing a wide variety of electronic warfare tools in the South China Sea, paying close attention to tools that disrupt electronic communications and radar systems.

This clear escalation in the development of electronic warfare and information warfare tools among adversaries is not lost on the United States. Now more than ever, the Pentagon and U.S. military feel the pressure of bringing the U.S.'s information tools up to speed and to the forefront of their strategies.

I. QANON DECODED - THE AWAKENING BEGINS

CULTIVATING WARFARE EXPERTS

As we mentioned above, information warfare truly starts with people. As much as the information war relies on people for development and growth, people need the information war and information warfare tactics to protect and prepare themselves for the future. Like we saw above, the information war is ongoing, growing faster than anyone can keep up, and our adversaries are more than on top of their game. Moreover, the information war has created the problem of how tech platforms and the government respond to information warfare operations while still maintaining free flow of ideas and free speech. It is no small feat, and it is challenging that private platforms deal with every day, which we will talk about in detail later on.

Much like the conclusion that the Pentagon came to, the general public needs information warfare tactics and warfare experts to deal with a massive influx of misinformation, fake news, media hoaxes, and more. The environment is changing. The attacks are getting more and more complex. Not to mention the attacks are affecting more than computer systems, they are affecting people too. Evidently, our framework for handling the information war is massively underdeveloped, which is why it is so essential. To have an underdeveloped information war strategy is better than no strategy at all.

Also, the need of information warfare is necessary to the people because it encourages integration with the government. Because the people are now being pulled into the information war, they are inevitable parts of the solution.

Lastly, the information war is necessary because it encourages the creation of a new generation of war experts. Information technology relies on the intelligence and skills of numerous people. Also, as more countries compete in the information war, more people are needed to explore evolutions in artificial intelligence, space travel, new energy, marine engineering, new materials and more. The demand for highly intelligent, skilled individuals is quite high in the information war. In a way, it creates a new industry built primarily for warfare support.

13
WHO MET Q?

TOM LEWIS

Tom Lewis wrote:

Q is Real

I am not Q; however, I have been asked to verify that QAnon and The Storm are quite real.

Why have I been asked? How can you trust me? I am not affiliated with QAnon, I am not a Trump supporter, I am not a Republican, nor am I a Democrat. My personal religious beliefs keep me from getting involved with politics. I am 47 and I have been faithful to my wife for 25 years. I do not smoke, drink, or vote. I have no agenda. But I have met Q.

I became acquainted with Q at a barbeque (no pun intended) at my Uncle's house in Branson Missouri. My Uncle and Q work together and are both Scotch drinkers. While I do not take part in politics, I do find Things of the World very interesting. Q and my uncle had partaken in a few drinks after which they told me a number of stories which I now know are facts.

I. QANON DECODED - THE AWAKENING BEGINS

Non-spoiler alert, I will not reveal any names, nor will I blow Q's cover. This is partially due to my integrity and partially due to fear for my safety and that of others.

Below are facts about Q:

1. Q is Caucasian

2. Q is a natural born US citizen

3. Q has been in military intelligence, though I do not know where he or my Uncle are currently employed

4. Q enjoys drinking a Scotch called Oban

5. Q is not a fan of Quentin Tarantino movies, I'm not sure why he made a point of telling me that

6. Q considers his health to be his number 1 priority

7. Q drives an American car

Below are facts about The Great Awakening/QAnon/The Storm:

1. Former high-level political figures are involved activities to undermine the current president

2. A few high-ranking members of the Legislative Branch of the government are involved in illegal practices which take advantage of American, Hispanic, and Asian children.

3. There is a secret religious organization that worships the Antichrist and its members are among very wealth and famous families. One of them was in a movie called Inferno. I do not believe it's Mr. Hanks. Nor do I believe he wanted to be in that movie.

4. Q's and a number of others have put their safety at risk in order to undermine what they consider to be Evil Forces.

I have seen proof of all the facts above through hacked emails and videos. I have been instructed to let you know these resources are available to you if you have basic detective and IT skills. I am not that computer literate. I can write emails, keep up with my grandkids on social media, and do my taxes. That's about it. But my Uncle said even I could find the evidence they showed me online if I followed their clues. He the instructed me to publish this on Amazon and give you the following clues:

A. 091120122140

B. Not whom you thought

C. Echo Delta Alabama

D. You are my sUNSHINE

I am publishing this under my real name, though my name is fairly common. Please do not attempt to contact me nor my family. I am publishing this because I believe the men and women involved with the movement are on the side of Good.

He was no part of this world nor am I.

14
GLOBAL ELITES OF THE NEW WORLD ORDER

A significant date in the creation of The New World Order occurred at a secret meeting in 1910, on Jekyll Island, Georgia. In attendance were a group of bankers and politicians. This meeting resulted in the transfer of power to create money from the U.S. government to a private group of bankers. In 1913, the Federal Reserve was created, the Rothschild banking cartel. The IMF (International Monetary Fund), is a Rothschild tool, a precursor of The New World Order, one world centralized banking system. These powerful and influential global bankers are planning for transformation from a cashless society to a digital payment system, where they will possess complete control, and can monitor every transaction. At the same time, they can focus on the destruction of real-world currencies. This will allow them to issue money that doesn't exist, creating impossible financial debt burdens upon the public masses. While in the background they continue to prosper accumulating remarkable wealth and power for themselves.

It has been claimed that the NWO elite and their corporate banks are now proceeding with steps to acquire the cryptocurrency market, so they can destroy any threat to their banking empire. They desire 100% control of every financial transaction that will be processed through their digital payment system. Once the world population is accustomed to this electronic payment system, it will become incredibly vulnerable to outages, glitches, or cyberattacks. They will be able to collapse the economy, make new laws to manipulate the public financially, through Congress. These elites control Congress through their lobbyists from their corporations, taking orders from them, using bribery, campaign donations, or blackmail of their personal scandals. This is why there is no oversight on Congress, no term limits, the Global elites need each player in Congress to fulfill their role to the NWO agenda. This final global economic system is intensifying, and accelerating a ban on cash throughout the world. Financially turning paper currency into digital currency makes it much easier for them to enslave the population.

The most powerful of these global elites are the Rothschilds and the Rockefellers. Their wealth is more than the entire wealth of the world's population, in control of our banking system and the Federal Reserve. There are 13 bloodline families that comprise this occult secret society known as the Illuminati, Bundy, Astor, Collins, DuPont, Freeman, Kennedy, Li, Onassis, Reynolds, Rockefeller, Rothschild, Russell, and Van Duyn. Their members are the corporate elite, politicians, world leaders, bankers, and celebrities. International organizations include the Bilderbergs, The Trilateral Commission, The World Health Organization, The United Nations, Council on Foreign Relations, and the Club of Rome, Big Pharma, and the Royal family of England, Queen Elizabeth II and the House of Windsor. These secret societies of the NWO collective are the Freemasons, Rosicrucians, Knights Templar, and the Vatican.

The Illuminati, a secret occult society, believe they are superior, in their wisdom and guidance for humanity, and those that have the money, rule the world and make the rules. With nothing but contempt for the poor, their NWO agenda is a platform of socialism, where the individual's rights are subservient to the state, where rights and powers are only granted through the state, not the individual. Their decisions cannot be questioned or challenged, they will tell us what to think, where to live and work, how many children we can have, every aspect of our lives will be controlled by them. World leaders are their puppets, and we are their sheep. Their goal is complete total dominion and control over the world, with no borders, and no national sovereignty. They create manipulation of the masses for distraction purposes such as identity politics, false flag attacks, race, paid protester groups, politics, and political correctness, and attempt to desensitize us to violence. The majority of the wars, political upheavals, and economic recessions and depressions are carefully masterminded by these elites.

They seek to destroy any class structure, everyone will be equally destitute, and absolve the family unit, where everyone serves the good of the collective. No personal property, firearms will be permitted. There will be world courts with a unified code of laws, one militarized police force, and one global economic system all under their control. One of their main objectives is to depopulate the world population from slightly over 7 billion to 500 million, a level they consider to be sustainable. By using the tools of vaccines, GMOS, bioengineered food, weather manipulation through HAARP, and geoengineered chemtrails, and new biometric technologies like Smart Dust, they are well on their way to achieving this goal. The New World Order Agenda includes a cashless society, a global surveillance network of implantable human microchips, a one world religion, occultism and persecution of Christians, and the brainwashing of children through the Common Core curriculum, where an individual's rights are subservient to the rights of the collective, in order to preserve the earth's resources.

Sometimes the truth can be very uncomfortable with many unpleasant realities, like you have awakened from a bad dream, but it is better to face reality, instead of being controlled and manipulated till the very end. To be informed, and therefore make your individual plans accordingly. These are people that are ruthless in achieving their agenda, and feel no remorse for their actions. They intend to complete their smart grid technology into smart cities where they claim it will improve efficiency quality, and everyone and everything will be connected to one electronic infrastructure.

From a biblical perspective, Christians believe that a cashless society is a fulfillment of Bible prophecy of the coming of the Antichrist. He is a global dictator that requires everyone on earth to receive a mark on the right hand or forehead, and those without this mark won't be able to buy or sell anything Revelation 13:16, 13:17. The technology now exists for the implementation of this mark, and speculation is rampant on what it might be, as the Antichrist would control every transaction in the world. Theories range on the "Mark of the Beast", from implantable microchips,

RFID chips, VeriChips, or perhaps visible tattoos, etc. The stage has been set for an electronic payment system that foreshadows the cashless society, and currently the majority of transactions are processed through a digital payment system of credit, debit, debit chip cards, and mobile phone payments. In the future, when the Antichrist seizes power, the final global economic system will already exist. The new technology will make paper currency obsolete, and there will be no choice.

This book has been a brief introduction into the origin of smart technologies, the smart grid, the future of biometrics, and the shift towards a cashless society. It defines The NWO agenda, with their ultimate goal, a one world totalitarian government with total control and dominion over mankind. I always encourage my readers to do their own intensive research, to arrive at their own conclusions. To sort through the propaganda, separating fact from fiction, and using a common sense approach in analyzing the situation, to assemble the pieces of the puzzle together, and see if it is probable or not.

Do you believe that the Global Elites have your best interests in mind, or are they perpetrating a "smart" technology grid to make them rulers over us and we their obedient servants? Are your smartphone and other smart devices truly your best friend, or an NWO tool to advance their agenda? These questions must be answered by each individual by being informed and prepared to make the necessary choices. At first, conspiracy theorists claim the switch to the cashless society will be voluntary as it is now, but in the final stage, it will be mandatory. Everyone will be forced to adhere to the one world government system, or lack the means to survive without food and shelter. They will tell us where to live, work, what to think, independent thought will be discouraged for the good of the collective. Our personal freedoms of speech, private property, the right to bear arms, will all be abolished. Their goal is for a drastically reduced unarmed, docile and compliant microchipped population.

The NWO distracts us with politics, protests, chaos in the world, and our love for our smartphones, and new technologies, so we will be unaware of their gradual indoctrination in our society. You will never hear from the media what is truly transpiring behind the scenes. They are totally controlled by the NWO, and we will hear and see only what they want us to know. Today's Hollywood movie themes are clues to the apocalyptic future they have set in motion for us, as they are in control of their production and Hollywood celebrities. They have no conscience or compassion for any human suffering or hardship imposed upon us by their actions.

Their sinister plot is already being implemented in the "Green New Deal", using smart green technologies to defeat the premise of global warming, which has not been factually proven. They want to eliminate cars, the fossil fuel industry, the limitation of meat. In fact, there is a great debate over climate change and global warming, with top scientists on both sides of the issue protesting their findings. The UN Agenda 21/2030 is also based on green technologies and sustainable development, employing smart technologies, where we will reside in human settlement zones. Resistance will lead to interment in a Fema Camp or worse, as the ends justifies the means for them. Are you willing to give up all your individual rights and liberties for these advanced new technologies? The Global Elites will continue to live their lives the way they always have, with no sacrifices, while our lives will never be the same. All of us will be equally poor, and unable to put up a rebellion against them.

Now is the time for awareness, to make a stand as one United States of America, not allowing their plan of tyranny, treachery and deception to completely infiltrate our country. They already believe they have won, as they get closer and closer to finalizing their tasks. There is still the opportunity to thwart their agenda as they will not be prepared for any unexpected surprises. Every individual should make the necessary preparations to protect themselves, their family and friends with provisions of emergency supplies, and a location for shelter purposes. For when they do attempt to enforce their goals, they will move quickly, not allowing any time for reprisals from the population. American freedom is priceless, cherished, and should always be preserved for posterity.

II. QANON UNLOCKED- SECRETS FROM THE SOURCE

INTRODUCTION

For those of you who have heard of QAnon, but only have a vague idea of what it is really all about, I'll provide a brief overview here.

In short form, QAnon is a conspiracy theory that alleges a vast, worldwide scheme by Evil Doers in the USA and abroad, known collectively as "the Deep State," to do lots of really bad things and keep doing them. There may also be a larger purpose or end game here— establishing the "New World Order" or some such—but it's not very clear. In fact, it seems (not surprisingly, when you look into the specifics) that the advocates for this theory can't quite agree on what the specific agenda of the Evil Doers is, other than to keep being really, really bad.

Fighting against the cabal of Evil Doers is a pair of heroes. The first of these great champions is Q, aka QAnon. Ostensibly a high-ranking member of the Trump administration with a military intelligence background, this nameless, faceless individual provides information—sporadically—via what are known as "drops." These are just coded pieces of text, called "crumbs," which further must be deciphered in order to have any meaning at all. Doing this are self-appointed Q interpreters, known as "bakers," who take the crumbs and cook them into something with meaning. Well, theoretically.

INTRODUCTION

Aiding Q in his selfless fight, tooth and nail against the Deep State, is our second hero: Donald J. Trump. Yep! He of the 10 days of golf per month, and 4-6 hours of TV watching and tweeting per day. Apparently, running the country and taking down a viciously powerful global cabal of Evil Doers doesn't take much time at all. Well, he has assured us he is "really smart" and a "stable genius," so this must be the proof.

The Storm (or something to that effect: mass arrests, uprisings, imposition of martial law, etc.) has been announced as immanent by Q multiple times, but has yet to actually materialize. Which I would argue is a very good thing, since the dreams of Q-oids sound fascistic and totally un-American to many, yours truly included.

In the broader sense, take any and all crazy, totally irresponsible, scurrilous, slanderous, outrageous claims you've ever heard anyone ever make, jumble them all together, add in baby mills, Satanism and human sacrifice, and then attribute it all to liberals—yes, bleeding heart liberals—and you now have QAnon in a nutshell.

I mean, I freely subscribe to the "conspiracy theory" which says Democrats (aka liberals), as a group, are completely incompetent. It's about the only "conspiracy" this group is traditionally capable of being a part of. The recent results of the 2018 midterms notwithstanding, the modern Dem Party has a stunning track record of snatching defeat from the jaws of victory. Witness the election that not only gave us the Man-Baby, but which put the GOP in charge of entire regions of the nation.

In summary, QAnon is, at best, an extremely dubious set of outrageous, unproven, slanderous "proofs" which, by the very nature of their delivery, are open to interpretation. Further, because many of them are so vague and ambiguous, it is relatively easy to make them align with known events, thereby providing "proof" for those who don't think too hard or delve too deeply into how ridiculous it all is.

You've probably searched the Internet and haven't found a reliable source that can answer your questions. There is no need to look any further; here you will find answers to your questions, in an orderly manner, and for beginners who have no idea about QAnon.

INTRODUCTION

Do not wait any longer, and keep reading, here we will teach you everything you need to discover and follow Q posts, and how to learn to read them. Thanks to the simple structure of the book, you will see that it helps you little by little to understand more deeply everything that surrounds us, and to realize that not everything is what it seems. You will learn to look at yourself critically.

WHO IS Q? IS TRUMP RELATED? WHERE CAN I READ HIS MESSAGES?

The QAnon movement did not start out with a bang. In fact, you can say that it only started with whispers. These whispers were done online on an imageboard that was frequented by what society considers as outcasts. These people were the perfect audience for Q because they are not your typical reader. These people are used to hoaxes so they are not easily swayed by what can be considered as crazy ramblings from someone pretending to have access to information that even the vice president of the United States may not have. After spending some time in the fringes, the QAnon movement began to seep into the mainstream.

Q silently emerged from the recesses of 4chan. This is an imageboard website where users can post anonymously. 4chan is divided into different boards that have their own content type and guidelines. It is important to note that this English-language site has been linked to internet activism and is the birthplace of many subcultures such as alt-right, Anonymous, and Project Chanology. The users of 4chan are the ones responsible for the creation and popularization of memes like Pedobear, lolcats, and Rick-rolling. These people have been described by The Guardian as "juvenile... brilliant... alarming".

Q's very first entry was posted under the "Mueller Investigation" thread. This was found on the board known as /pol/. This first entry was logged on October 28, 2017. Q proceeded to post on various threads before the emergence of a new thread – Breadcrumbs - Q Clearance Patriot.

Q has long since grown to be a huge phenomenon, not just in the US but all over the world. Millions of people wait for his breadcrumbs and hundreds diligently do their research in order to analyze and interpret what Q means. As of 2019, there are over a thousand articles written about QAnon and the movement. Most that are written about Q and his followers are hostile towards Q and the people who believe in his drops.

Some are dismissive and see the QAnon movement as conspiracy theorists who will grab at straws. Still, others believe in what Q has to say and devote themselves to spreading his words. They tweet and retweet his posts. They make video analysis on every breadcrumb so that anybody who is interested in learning about Q and his truths understands what is happening. They share these videos, blogs, and tweets on Facebook so that they can reach more people. The shares on social media are staggering. Conspiracy theory or not, nobody can deny that Q has touched and influenced millions of lives. And the person that Q may have helped the most is President Trump. Without Q's help, a lot of his supporters may have already given up on this seemingly clueless leader.

The Anon in the term "QAnon" refers to the individual Q, who remains anonymous to this day, and the countless nameless supporters of this individual. While a lot of alternate theories rise and fall in the world of 4Chan, QAnon managed to stay alive for nearly two years. Why is this? IS it because Q knew how to give his audience just enough to keep their interests? Or is because people are awake enough to see that the person at the other end knows his stuff, unlike other theorists?

Followers wait for Q's entries to be posted. They believe that Q is using the website to secretly keep the public abreast of President Trump's masterplan in eliminating the members and the leaders of the Deep State. When people started questioning whether Q really existed and whether he was really an insider, he showed the readers proof that he was with the President on Air Force One by posting a blurry picture of a few islands. This coincided with Trump's trip to Asia.

What does Q post? He reveals top-secret details in clue form. Eventually, these clues were labeled as "breadcrumbs". It was the readers on 4Chan who became the "bakers" of Q – the ones who put together the "breadcrumbs" that was posted and turned it into a "dough". The breadcrumbs are very hard to interpret as they appear to be a cross between ransom note and poetry. As an example, look at what Q posted in June of 2018.

After the bakers studied the dropped crumbs, they put their own spin to it and post it on their individual accounts. They talk about it on Reddit. They post videos of their interpretation on YouTube. They share links of other bakers' analysis on Facebook. This is how the QAnon movement grew.

❦ 2 ❦
HOW TO DECIPHER Q'S DROPS?

Part of Q's mission involves the exposure of global corruption. Naturally, those who commit criminal acts would not want their deeds exposed. That makes Q an enemy of the rich and powerful, and a target for retaliation. As a potential target of powerful people, if he were wise, he would want to avoid being identified. One way to conceal your identity from corrupt people would be to post anonymously on the internet. People have been doing that for years on the internet message boards called 4chan and 8chan (sometimes called the chans).

Q initially posted on the 4chan load up named politically off base (once in a while called/pol/). That board was picked for some particular reasons. 4chan clients can stay unknown, which is the reason government representatives once in a while use it to drop data about open defilement. The board is frequented by PC nerds who are skilled at uniting information from articles, recordings, open records, and different sources. By day, mysterious clients (likewise called anons or autists) fill in as frameworks experts, coders, and game fashioners. Around evening time, they inquire about the pieces of information individuals drop, without the information on their managers, and without realizing who composed the posts they're examining. (The term autist, as utilized on message sheets like 4chan, doesn't derive that an individual has chemical imbalance. Rather, it's a slang term that depicts indi-

II. QANON UNLOCKED- SECRETS FROM THE SOURCE

viduals with the capacity to be hyper focused as they process a lot of data).

Anons have inquired about posts from insight network insiders (both genuine and phony) for quite a long time. Individuals consistently demonstrate up on the chans professing to be a specialist from the CIA or another insight office. They'll profess to have insider data on an examination or anticipate the capture of a celebrated individual, and as a rule, they're never gotten notification from again. Their expectations only occasionally work out as expected on the grounds that a great many people professing to be insight insiders are fakes. Managing fakes has made the anons a bored parcel. They'll expect a heap of verification before they'll purchase your "insight insider" story. On the chans, a fake is additionally called a LARP (or Live Action Role Player). LARP shows that the culprit of the misrepresentation is simply showcasing a job.

Q has figured out how to persuade anons of his authenticity, yet prevailing press outlets haven't tried to disclose this to their pursuers. In the numerous articles they've composed attempting to ruin Q, journalists will in general depict anons as fierce and simple fanatics. (This has not been my experience; I've seen them as profoundly insightful and systematic. In spite of the fact that they can be enthusiastic about their convictions, the anons who follow Q don't underwrite brutality.) After a huge number of negative articles had been distributed about Q and the anons close to the finish of July 2018, one of the anons posted the accompanying message:

Mysterious • Jul 30 2018 ARTICLES ABOUT QWHY DO THEY NEVER ASK THE ANONS WHY they're HERE?REAL ANON'S are here as we follow the EVIDENCE (archived evident proof), we are building the reality of our HISTORY so we will uncover and disassemble the debasement that has PLAGUED our reality for millennia. I welcome any distribution to print this as an announcement of certainty from an ACTUAL ANON. we do not mention to YOU what to think or the way to FEEL a few theme. WE essentially burrow for TRUTH and afterward PRESENT what we discover so it tends to be examined by our PEERS and further corroborated. the selection to understand what we've discovered, checked and introduced is completely up to YOU. Introducing us add a fashion to infer WE are a kind of faction, shows the planet how degenerate the MAINSTREAM MEDIA has become. WE aren't about brutality, disruption or control. WE are just giving FACT based data freed from charge to the planet .WWG1WGAFeel liberal to SHARE End

Q reacted to the anon:

National security laws confine the data government authorities can give to people in general. Ordered data is untouchable, however there is an abundance of significant data that is open source. Actually, open source data is essential to such an extent that in 2005, the Office of the Director of National Intelligence (ODNI) made the Director of National Intelligence Open Source Center (OSC). The OSC is entrusted with improving the accessibility of open sources to insight officials and other government authorities. Similarly, that the OSC gives non-arranged data to its customers, Q furnishes his pursuers with data that is openly accessible to people in general and which, whenever united and accurately deciphered, illustrates what might some way or another require characterized data to comprehend.

Q Can Be Difficult to Understand

Numerous individuals discover Q's posts astounding. There are various purposes behind that. The principal reason is that Q utilizes a strategy for guidance that is once in a while utilized today. In the second 50% of the fifth century BC, critics were instructors who utilized way of thinking and talk to engage, dazzle, or convince their crowd to acknowledge a perspective. The Greek savant Socrates utilized an alternate way to deal with educating. The Socratic strategy is a type of helpful contentious exchange between people. The exchanging posing and replying of inquiries is utilized to compel basic reasoning, the investigation of thoughts, and the assessment of fundamental presuppositions. The Socratic technique prompts speculation end; better theories develop by consistently recognizing and dispensing with frail ones or ones that lead to logical inconsistencies. Normally, a progression of inquiries is presented that are planned as trial of rationale and reality. These inquiries help an individual find their fundamental convictions about some subject and distinguish convictions that ought to be disposed of.

We live in a culture today where correspondents put down articles and account interviews passing on their comprehension of an offered subject to us. It's increasingly similar to a monolog; there is no discussion included. There is no assessment of fundamental convictions. There is no trying of rationale or examination of the authentic premise of explanations. We're required to acknowledge the realities as they are given to us by the moderator without addressing them. The moderator doesn't only let us know "the realities." They additionally relegate importance to the realities. Whoever appoints importance to data decides the open account regarding that matter. The media will in general decipher data such that bolsters an ideological conviction framework. In the event that you acknowledge an individual's introduction of realities, you're bound to acknowledge their ideological convictions.

As opposed to the model of the predominant press, Q utilizes the Socratic strategy. Utilizing questions, he'll look at our present convictions on a given subject. He'll inquire as to whether our conviction is legitimate, at that point drop indicates about realities we might not have revealed, and propose an elective theory. He may give a connect to

a report and urge us to accomplish more research. The data we need is freely accessible. We're allowed to lead our exploration in the manner we need. We're additionally allowed to decipher the data anyway we need. We should arrive at our own decisions since Q downplays his understandings. For some, individuals, investigating for themselves, having an independent mind, and believing their own decisions can make following Q troublesome. At the point when you're acclimated with somebody mentioning to you what to figure, thinking for yourself can be a difficult change.

In spite of the fact that Q has an ideological structure that is focused on opportunity and equity, he gives data in a way that can be deciphered anyway one picks. To be sure, a typical analysis of Q is that his messages don't give any genuine importance since they can be deciphered in for all intents and purposes any way possible. The way that we're allowed to decipher Q's data anyway we pick doesn't mean there are no set-in stone answers. Q set up an arrangement of correspondence where specialists can request intimations or post the discoveries of their examination and have hypotheses checked. Numerous individuals have gotten affirmation or help from Q basically by posting their work on Twitter. Q may affirm our hypothesis similar to the case in this arrangement of posts from December 22nd and 23rd, 2017.

Dec 22 2017

How did NK abruptly have scaled down nukes upon POTUS getting to work?

What was expressed during Hussein's term by offices?

How did NK unexpectedly get missile direction top?

What is influence?

Characterize prisoner.

Their last expectation!

Q

An anon inquired as to why the letter "I" was absent from "rocket" in the above post.

Mysterious • Dec 23 2017

Q posts missing letter "I" are markers?

Q reacted with a piece of information:

What rocket terminated today?

[i]

Message sent.

Q

An anon reacted, taking note of that SpaceX had as of late propelled its Falcon 9 rocket to convey a variety of satellites for Iridium Communications.

Mysterious

Iridium?

Q affirmed the missing letter "I" in his posts was a sign about the Iridium satellites and said future news would open more data.

Future news will open a greater amount of the message.

Missing [i] affirmed.

Q

Exploring the hints gave by Q is tedious work, yet I've discovered that doing my own examination, coming to an obvious conclusion, and arriving at my own decisions encourages me comprehend recorded and recent developments in a progressively complete manner.

LEARNING THE LINGO OF THE CHANS

Conversations on 4chan, 8chan, and 8kun are hosted on various subdomains called boards. Each board hosts discussions on a particular topic. The boards are run by volunteers (board volunteers or BVs) who create and moderate conversations (threads). Board volunteers are sometimes called bakers. The threads are called breads. When a baker creates a new thread, they're said to be "baking a bread." A single comment in a thread is called a crumb. Helpful information on a topic is called sauce. The term sauce is derived from the word "source." If a point is made that isn't common knowledge, others will naturally ask for the source (sauce) of the information.

Q first began posting on the 4chan board, politically incorrect (/pol/), on October 28th, 2017. One problem with /pol/ is the high amount of traffic it receives. Some users are interested in participating in open discussions and research but many users are trolls and shills. Trolls and shills aren't interested in fruitful discussions. They derail conversations with pointless objections and oppose whatever idea is being discussed. Some people are paid to do this. Q's posts on 4chan were swarmed by trolls and shills which made it difficult for serious discussions to take place. One month after Q began posting, his threads had drawn enough opposition that the decision was made to move to 8chan which receives less traffic. 8chan was used by people around the globe to communicate on whatever subjects they want. Some users live in countries where freedom of speech is severely restricted. Many people are shocked to see nudity when they first visit these message boards. Jim Watkins, the owner of 8chan and 8kun, is a free speech advocate. If content isn't explicitly illegal according to U.S. law, he allows it to be posted.

❧ 3 ❧
THE TENTACLES OF THE DEEP STATE

THE POLITICALLY PURPORTED TRUTH

That general society has gotten disappointed and careful about steady Armageddon media reports and news inclusion that hold fast to corporate plans, is an obtrusive modest representation of the truth — individuals see their reality changing and they need to comprehend what's going on, and why. They need to be educated, to along these lines set themselves up. They need the opportunity to settle on taught decisions, rather than being determined what to do by the very people and organizations that continually lie and trick, the very foundations at the base of all the tumult.

Even with MSM disinformation (CH 7 and 36), the site Final Wake Up Call is autonomous and keeps on conveying fundamental and convenient data. 650 We are appreciative for the contribution of up and coming editors, donors, volunteers, and pursuers' responses in assisting with completing this undertaking of truth dispersal. The input from our pursuers is a significant wellspring of consolation and inspiration for continuation. Shortening the tide of disinformation being siphoned out by ground-breaking and very much supported prevailing press, is a significant test.

II. QANON UNLOCKED- SECRETS FROM THE SOURCE

The control of the US and of worldwide legislative issues by the wealthiest families on earth, is practiced in a fantastic, significant and surreptitious way. This control started in Europe and has had a progression which will be followed back to when the investors found it had been more productive to supply credits to governments than to destitute people (CH 2). These financial families and their docile recipients have gone to possess most vital organizations (CH 7) over the 2 centuries, during which era they need subtly and progressively sorted out themselves as controllers of governments worldwide and as mediators of war and harmony.

Except if individuals completely get this, they're going to be unable to know the real purposes behind the 2 universal wars and therefore the approaching arranged Third World War, a war that's practically bound to start as an outcome of the US endeavor – with the guide of the EU politburo (CH 40) - to seize and control Central Asia. the most answer is for the U.S. also, the EU to ease off – something the individuals of the USA, the EU, and therefore the whole world actually need, yet not the force elites.

Be that because it may, the us has given the planet two options: war to shield the US Dollar, as against working with the Eastern Alliance towards the execution of another Gold Standard.

In spite of, or even on account of the irate endeavors of the world's Machiavellian destroyers, humankind is awakening. there's huge advancement being made in uncovering the progressing fierce Gaza eradication, the mass disclosures of HAARP's climate controls, the phony heating mantra – as lately modified into the global climate change mantra, Chemtrails harming the air and other neo-logical attacks, the moderate murder of humankind through toxin bound antibodies, even as the weaponization of pharmaceuticals and pharmaceutical methodology, the grievous impacts of EMFs (Electro Magnetic Fields) from different sources, GMO food control, structural RTF reconnaissance and observing, and at the up front, the obviously phony, initiated worldwide wars and therefore the militarization of society on the loose.

Try to not let these detestable practices occur or proceed, and guard against clear challenges in belief system losing you course. There's nothing level about this playing field and therefore the MSM mass story is an amazingly persuading publicity apparatus, initiated by the force world class. Try to not attempt to hear it out. depend upon the astuteness of your heart, acumen of the mind, insight, and presence of mind. Begin counseling elective news sources. The Illuminati's just weapon is our assent, whereby we respect their falsehoods. Disinformation fills a couple of needs, the foremost treacherous of which is that the presentation of uncertainty into your ardent feelings with reference to reality with regards to what's clearly occurring before you. Saving the mass psyche in check is basic for the satisfaction of their mystery motivation. The conventions of Sion which they follow, clarify that the target of worldwide control are going to be cultivated by controlling how the open thinks, by observing what they see and hear; by making new clashes or renovating old requests; by spreading craving, destitution, and plague; and by alluring and diverting the young. "By all of those techniques, we'll so wear out the countries that they're going to be compelled to supply us global control," broadcast the Illuminati. Peruse the Protocols 651 to perceive what more is coming.

Today, an ever increasing number of individuals around the world are awakening to the recently developing reality, with the understanding that what has been instructed verifiably, mingled and what we have been raised to accept politically as the fact of the matter, is a simple case of through and through horse crap.

Patterns and surveys lately have reported this move in perspective cognizance, reliably demonstrating a developing doubt of governments in both the US and Europe and to a developing degree in numerous nations of the world. A survey from January this year found that about two out of three doubt their legislature and another survey from April 2014 demonstrates three out of four accept their lawmakers are degenerate. Last October Pew Research Center found out that more than four out of five don't confide in their own legislature at all or if nothing else more often than not, a close to unequaled elevated level in the estimation of government doubt.

EUROPEANS NEED TO DISPOSE OF THE EUROPEAN UNION

EU parliamentary decisions were a finished and articulate disappointment for the European Union, with the point of turning into "the following

II. QANON UNLOCKED- SECRETS FROM THE SOURCE

United States of Europe," a flooding reaction of the eager enemy of EU voters from all over Europe sent periphery components from both the left and right to Brussels, with the particular plan to dispose of the European Union for the last time.

The voters' fury was heard with respect to the stale economy of France, the grimness vigilant Greeks, uneasiness in Denmark, right to Britain. A solid push for Ireland to quit the EU is developing. Numerous inhabitants, particularly in southern Europe were the hardest-hit countries, with serious grimness measures being forced by the almighty Germany, which is being accused for the monetary discomfort.

Oil-rich Scotland has even started to lead the pack in a dissident development, looking for autonomy from Britain. Cataluña in Spain looked for and decided in favor of freedom that has been obstructed by the Madrid government. Pais Vasco (Basque Country) in northern Spain idem dito. - Many Europeans have communicated hatred for large governments, which they fault for their high joblessness and bombed approaches, which have been seen as deficient in meeting their confined needs. Past the US and Europe, more residents around the world are becoming progressively furious with their chosen authorities, understanding that the government officials' sole need is to serve the necessities of their oligarch manikin aces, rather than the requirements of their own kin.

Russia-Bashing

U.S. President Barack Obama's war against Russia isn't just making Russia collaborate all the more unequivocally with the different BRICS nations to break the U.S. dollar's rule as the worldwide hold cash, but on the other hand it's pushing Russian President Vladimir Putin's endorsement rating higher, with work numbers in Russia taking off week after week and an ever-developing pace of certainty of the Russian individuals in their own Government.

The Ukrainian system, introduced by the U.S, has deliberately closed off any entrance of legitimate 'news' media into Donetsk - the star Russian eastern part – along these lines removing all covering the phosphor-shelling slaughter. Anybody despite everything hanging tight for the 'news' media to advise them about this firebombing, will most likely need to hold up until everybody is dead, before they stir to reality with regards to these violations. Actually, nobody cares, on the grounds that the more it takes, the less significant the 'news' will be — by then it will be history. The wonder of whether the casualties will be depicted as thoughtful in the history books, relies upon which side at last composes the history books on this war.

The illuminati are Satanists. They don't cry tears over a huge number of individuals in south-eastern Ukraine who are either being killed, or, more than likely escaping into exile camps inside Russia, all purposefully executed by individuals that the west has prepared and is financing, while at the same time being brought under psyche control. All trained activities are executed by the mystery plan, as spread out in the Protocols. For everybody in the western world, the applied assents with respect to Russia are deplorable for the entire economy on the two sides, explicitly Russia and the EU.

4
THE PEOPLE BEHIND THE DEEP STATE

When Obama set up the Iran deal and sent them billions of dollars, I couldn't stand by and watch any more. He was selling out the country to sworn enemies, and no one was saying a thing.

"I'm going to do it, John. I have no choice. I guess I knew I would have to since that day Obama flew Air Force One low over Manhattan and frightened people with his new power. All these years of his lies and deceit, and Hillary's personal agenda, have run America down. I want to make my country great again, as it was when we were prosperous, proud, and respected. I have no choice."

"You won't see me or know me," he said. "I'll be at your rallies and listen to every speech, and so will Carolyn. The millions who attend your inauguration will include me and my family. And when you finally get to remove the traitors and as many bribed people as you can, I'll reclaim my family name and stand beside you."

I rode the escalator to the lobby of Trump Tower and announced my candidacy, going up against 16 so called Republican hopefuls, and for the first time in my life, not being sure I could win.

MR. BABYLON

I wished it was John who was running. I wished his father had never been murdered. I wished that the American people had never elected Obama or considered Hillary a viable candidate.

I knew my conversations with John would have to end. As a candidate, all of my communications would be scrutinized and we couldn't risk exposing him.

He was right about my tax returns. One of the first battles was about my tax returns. I was thankful for the IRS audit that kept them out of the public eye. I didn't need or want questions about the little corporation named Barin.

It was a long and sometimes nasty campaign. Hillary's arrogance and belief that enough fraud was in place for her win, angered me and kept me going.

On Inauguration Day, I quietly looked for John among the millions, and during the State of the Union, I thought I felt him somewhere in the balcony.

I checked my followers on Twitter and wondered which one was him. Neither of us trusted social media enough to expose his name or presence in any form.

I visited the graves of his father and uncle and thought of Jackie's love for her children. Once or twice, I thought I saw his smile beneath a beard, and once or twice I thought a handshake was his. I always felt him near me, and as I proceeded to do what was right for America, the thought of him coming back gave me some of the strength to keep fighting for the people.

Suddenly, Twitter and Facebook came alive with threads from someone named Q. It was my son who alerted me to the tweets and information. Q and QAnon became immediately popular with so many who also followed me. His tweets were most often questioning with urgent messages to people to connect the dots, do the research, and find the answers.

When he began saying, "trust the plan," I knew John was somehow connected, and even I had to remember to trust the plan.

The media thought it was a hoax, and Twitter tried to shut him down, but I checked every day to see what was being said and how much people were learning. To do what was necessary to "drain the swamp," many people embedded in the agencies around me had to be arrested, indicted, and convicted. Hillary had to be marginalized or jailed, and the CIA and FBI had to be scrubbed.

It wasn't going to be a quick fix, and I knew I would be attacked from every side. When I needed to feel support for what I was doing, I scheduled a rally or a speech that would bring the energy of the people back to me.

Assassination attempts were rampant and my wife and son were being threatened daily, but I was alerted to all attempts by those around me who were loyal to the country, and also by the tweets from Q. He would say, "POTUS is safe," and I'd know the right people were there to protect me.

I forged ahead with the plan, running into obstruction everywhere, but still managing to slowly make the changes necessary. Obama's presidency had been a Coup d'état, many people not realizing that their country had been taken over or that we were in a war. I had to do what was right for the people, and what was right for America.

"When everything is in place, and only when it is, forge ahead."

John had managed to send a tweet without exposing himself, and I felt re-energized. When I met with Kim Jung Un, I knew it was right. And when Putin gave me a soccer ball and said the ball was now in my court, I was certain almost everything was in place.

Then, during a short press event about Russia, the lights went out for several seconds. When they came back on, I knew I had the full faith and support of everyone who would be involved in bringing America back, and I knew it wouldn't be long before I could shake the hand of the man who had helped me through it all.

Q, if you're out there and can hear me, we're ready and God is with us. The people are awakened. God bless America.

THE EPSTEIN CASE AND HIS FAMOUS CONNECTIONS

Allegations against Epstein

The first allegation against Jeffrey Epstein came in March 2005 when a woman informed the Palm Beach Police Department in Florida about an older girl taking her 14-year old stepdaughter to Epstein's mansion. The woman informed that her stepdaughter was offered $300 for stripping and massaging Epstein. The woman also stated that her daughter had apparently undressed although leaving Epstein's mansion wearing her underwear. Following the allegations, police started an undercover investigation of Epstein that spanned for 13 months. The FBI also participated in the investigation after a short gap.

Abuse of underage girls

The police subsequently uncovered evidence that allegedly tied up Epstein with payments to many girls for engaging in sexual acts with him. The concerns of Epstein abusing underage girls are evident in the interviews with alleged victims and the witnesses under oath as well as a high school transcript alongside certain items found in the trash and home of Epstein. The police correlated all these evidences to find out that almost all the girls who were sexually harassed by Jeffrey Epstein were under 18 years of age. Evidence also suggested that the youngest victim was 14 years old and the majority of the victims were under the age of 16 years. The police also came up with more substantiating evidence regarding the involvement of Epstein in abuse of underage girls upon searching his home. The police found two hidden cameras in Epstein's house along with many photos of girls all over the house. The police also found that some of the girls in the photos found in Epstein's house had been interviewed during their investigation process. According to statements of one of the former employees of Epstein, Epstein used to receive massages for at least three times a day. Finally, the FBI compiled a report stating that 34 minors were confirmed for their allegations of sexual abuse by Epstein and the proof was evident in corroborating details. The number of confirmed minors eligible for restitution, according to the FBI was increased to 40 in the non-prosecution agreement (NPA).

Pedophilia

Epstein was found to be involved in the abuse of underage girls through the police investigation. Also, he was also found to be involved in pedophilia according to investigations. The police chief at the time of the investigation, Michael Reiter, stated that there were over 50 girls and one boy who had allegations of sexual abuse by Jeffrey Epstein. However, the concerns of pedophilia came into concern when allegations of 12-year-old triplets brought in from France on the occasion of Epstein's birthday surfaced. Obviously, sexual abuse of underage girls can also be classified as pedophilia, but Epstein did not have any such boundaries. The 12-year-old triplets in question here were sexually abused and flown back to France the next day. The investigation findings also indicated that many underage girls were brought in from South America, Europe, and former Soviet Union countries. The Palm Beach police filed a probable cause affidavit in May 2006 which stated that Epstein should be charged with four counts of unlawful sex with minors as well as one instance of sexual abuse.

Famous Connections

In many of the victim and witness testimonies, one fact appears explicitly visible! What is that? Epstein escaped justice for quite a long time, and that is definitely a fact. Look at the treatment he received after being convicted as a sex offender and sentenced to 18 months in prison. Epstein was placed in a private wing of the Palm Beach County Stockade instead of the state prison that is the usual place where convicted sex offenders in

Florida are housed. After three and a half months, he was allowed to leave jail for around 12 hours a day for 6 days a week on 'work release.' Epstein was released after 13 months of 'prison sentence' for a year of probation on house arrest. However, the 'house arrest' also allowed Epstein to take numerous trips to his residences in the US Virgin Islands and Manhattan. These events clearly suggest that Epstein was not just a man of money but also a man with some powerful contacts. Epstein had a spectacular list of friends belonging to the elite class of society. So, let us take note of some of the important names that have been associated prominently with Jeffrey Epstein. One important fact to keep in mind here is that a majority of Epstein's contacts denied any form of involvement with him after allegations of sexual abuse and trafficking on Epstein surfaced in 2005.

Bill Clinton

The contact of Epstein with former US President, Bill Clinton, is one of the hot topics currently on the table for journalists and conspiracy theorists following Epstein's death. Epstein visited the White House and supposedly met Bill Clinton for the first time at a donor event during the presidency of Bill Clinton. Epstein is reported to have had meetings with a White House aide many times. After the end of Bill Clinton's presidency in 2001, the contact between Epstein and Clinton grew stronger.

Clinton was in a new stage of his career and was driven to travel the world and launch many philanthropic activities. Clinton had to hang out with celebrities and rich people during this time and make huge sums of money. According to a 2002 New York magazine profile, Clinton was attracted to Epstein solely for his plane. Clinton's aide Doug Band mediated the meeting between Bill Clinton and Jeffrey Epstein. In September 2002, Epstein took Clinton along with actors Kevin Spacey and Chris Tucker on his private jet for a tour of five African countries. Subsequently, Bill Clinton was also with Epstein on many other trips such as another trip to Africa, one to Asia and one to Europe. These statements are confirmed by the spokesperson for Clinton, Angel Urena. Clinton's team has also clarified in the past that Clinton's trips with Epstein were primarily about democratization, citizen service, fighting against HIV/AIDS and empowering the poor.

Clinton was accompanied by Secret Service agents and his security detail at all times on his flights with Epstein. Clinton's spokesperson clearly stated that the trips were meant to forward the work of Clinton Foundation. Bill Clinton had commented about Epstein to the New York Magazine through a spokesperson. Clinton stated that Epstein was a highly successful financier as well as a committed philanthropist. Clinton had also added that Epstein had a keen sense of global markets along with comprehensive knowledge about 21st-century science. One of the alleged victims of Epstein, Virginia Giuffre, also stated that she had seen Clinton on the Little St. James Island, the private island of Jeffrey Epstein. However, Giuffre also stated that she never had sexual relations with Clinton. She also added that she had never seen Clinton having sexual relations with anyone on the island. The spokesperson for Clinton, Angel Urena, stated that Clinton had never visited Epstein's ranch in New Mexico, his residence in Florida or his private island in Little St. James.

Prince Andrew

Another notable name that comes up frequently among the mentions of notable and influential friends of Epstein is the Duke of York, Prince Andrew. A report states that their friendship began in 1999 when they met each other through Ghislaine Maxwell, who is also a renowned British socialite. The relationship of Epstein with other members of the royal family is not known. However, Prince Andrew was photographed walking with Jeffrey Epstein in Central Park in 2010 after Epstein had finished his prison sentence. In a recent statement released on August 24, 2019, Prince Andrew has claimed that he stayed at many of the properties owned by Epstein. He also added that he did not meet with Epstein very often and saw him only once or twice in a year. Epstein has also been connected to Prince Andrew through the latter's ex-wide Sarah Ferguson. According to a report by the Telegraph in 2011, Epstein had paid £15,000 to the former personal assistant of Sarah Ferguson based on the orders of the Duke of York. The payment was supposedly responsible for a wider restructuring of Sarah's debts worth £5 million. Sarah Ferguson has apologized for her involvement with Epstein and has confirmed that she will repay the money and also stated that the payment was facilitated by her ex-husband, i.e., Prince Andrew.

Furthermore, unlike many other leaders who issued statements denying any form of involvement with Epstein, Prince Andrew did not speak anything on the matter for many weeks. However, recent statements were issued by the Buckingham Palace in August 2019 that was related to the relationship between Prince Andrew and Epstein. Prince Andrew also admitted recently that he had committed a mistake and an error by spending time with Epstein in 2010 even after his conviction as a sex offender.

The official statement by the Buckingham Palace also includes the statement of Prince Andrew in which he claims to have never seen, witnessed, or suspected any form of behavior that led to Epstein's arrest and conviction. The Buckingham Palace had published two official statements regarding Prince Andrew's involvement with Epstein. The most notable point of association between Prince Andrew and Epstein arises from the allegations of notable Epstein accuser, Virginia Giuffre. Giuffre claimed in court documents that she was forced to have sex with Prince Andrew at the age of 17 years by Epstein. She has also claimed that she had sex with Prince Andrew on three different occasions. Therefore, Prince Andrew appears to be another elite member in the network and friends of Epstein who denied contacts with him after his involvement in the sexual offense allegations.

Others

Epstein also had many other notable names in his network and his friend circle. One of the prominent names is the CEO of L Brands, Les Wexner. Epstein managed finances for Wexner and reportedly, he is the only listed client of Epstein's own financial consultancy firm. Wexner actually purchased Even the Manhattan residence of Epstein in 1989 through a trust. After Wexner moved to Ohio with his wife, Abigail Koppel, in 1996, the ownership of the house was transferred to Epstein in 2011 for just $0. However, according to a recent statement by an L Brands spokesperson, Wexner had severed all contacts with Epstein after firing him from the position of finance manager over a decade ago.

The different names in Epstein's network have some sort of connection to Epstein at some or the other point. While the exact nature of the relationships between Epstein and his network of friends is not clear, mainstream media reports have associated Jeffrey Epstein with some top names in the world. Some of his notable contacts include Michael Jackson, Rupert Murdoch, Katie Couric, the Kennedys, the Rockefellers, Michael Bloomberg, the Rothschilds, Alec Baldwin, Kevin Spacey, Chris Tucker, Richard Branson, and Woody Allen among others. He also had friendly ties with Israeli prime minister Ehud Barak, British prime minister Tony Blair and the Saudi Arabian crown prince Mohammed Bin Salman. These names speak a lot about the type of power Epstein enjoyed during his lifetime.

6
THE STORM IS COMING: THE 2020'S DECADE

"The 'cabal' has owned the current banking system since before World War II." "Q" explained. "As such, all transactions must travel through 'cabal central' banks, where the 'cabal gray men' have the last 'say' over what will be done with the money. Over the last several decades, nothing happens in the banking business unless the 'gray men' approve it."

"So, if they control the 'money supply' as well as the destination, what chance do we have to take back our world?" Sheryl asked. "Even if we assassinate every last "cabal banker" in the world, they still control the 'system' itself. They control the SWIFT transfer systems. Right?"

"You are so right, my dear!" "Q" proclaimed. "Unless we can wrestle control of the SWIFT banking transfer system and its 'codes', we will never be able to overcome their power over our lives."

"Then what is the answer?" Rami asked. "You must have already figured this problem out? Right?"

"Yes," Caroline replied. "It has to do with a completely new banking control system which involves 'Quantum control banking', an 'A.I.' banking system. It will solve all the current banking problems, and together with the 'Manna World Holding Trust', a new world will be created."

II. QANON UNLOCKED- SECRETS FROM THE SOURCE

"How in the world could we ever wrestle control from these people?" Sheryl asked. "It seems an impossible situation!"

"You are so correct." "Q" replied. "But that which is impossible for man is quite possible for God."

"God raises up the necessary "Master" from every realm of His Kingdom when they are needed the most." Caroline answered. "In this case, a miracle occurred which ultimately led to a takeover of the various Trusts themselves."

"Throughout time, "Q" explained, "the various 'Trusts' owned by the cabal, were officiated over by a single Trustee, who was responsible to transfer such funds to the locations requested by the Cabal leaders. As time passed, control passed to a very special 'agent' of the Almighty Creator; this woman is now simply known as 'Kim'; her formal name is 'Kim Gauguin', a 7th generation Rothschild!"

"Kim has turned out to be the actual savior of this planet," Caroline said. "She became sole Trustee in 2015, and immediately began to accumulate all the various Trusts into one giant trust, which is now described as the 'Manna World Holding Trust'. Kim has decided to refuse to use these funds on behalf of the Rothschild cabal."

"Instead," "Q" explained with great delight, "Kim has decided to use the giant Trust funds for the betterment of the human race. She has also taken the funds out of the 'SWIFT' system of banking, wherein the 'cabal bankers' would have continued to maintain control over the use of the funds. Instead Kim has chosen to use a new and improved 'Quantum A.I.' Aided banking system. No other person in the world has access to this money; Kim's action will lead directly to the bankruptcy of all the 'cabal central banks', including the 12 Federal Reserve Banks in the United States."

"Wow", Rami exclaimed. "That is the greatest news we have ever heard. Why is that we have never heard of such a thing?"

"Not many people understand how the banking systems works;" Caroline replied. "But this is a 'game-changer' for the world.

"So, we do not need to worry about the banking system?" Sheryl asked. "Without their access to money, what will the 'cabal' do to maintain their control?"

"They are still a powerful group," "Q" announced. "They still have their 'armies' in Europe (NATO), and they have their 'assassins', and their access to plenty of nuclear weapons."

"The U.S. new Quantum banking system will be handled by the Treasury Department, which will be centered in Reno, Nevada." Caroline added. "The Internal Revenue will be dismantled and their employees moved to the Treasure Department. The Federal Reserve assets will be taken over by the Treasure Department, and the 'cabal bankers' will be escorted out of the country."

"Kim has been a God-send", "Q" announced. "She will ultimately transfer appropriate moneys to every country in a fair honest manner, as she will do to the United States. Since our country will no longer be giving 'all' of our taxes to the 'cabal bankers', the United States will become a very wealthy country, and all 'income taxes' will be eliminated. Further, Kim will transfer 'trillions' of dollars to help America begin to rebuild our crumbling infrastructure. The future of the United States, as well as the world, has never been brighter."

"Wow" Rami exclaimed. "Now all we need to do is to eliminate the 'bad actors' in our government, business community, media and entertainment system. Have all of those individuals been identified?"

"Funny you should ask about that!" "Q" exclaimed. "That is what we will discuss right now."

"The President refused to deal with the Vatican money representative Cardinal Pell," Caroline explained. "All the money in the world would never convince Trump to make a 'deal with the devil'. As soon as he was elected, Trump decided to attack a number of 'dark players' in our nation. He started with those persons involved in the 'pedophile world' together with those involved in 'human trafficking'. It is this group who provide the young children and woman which the alien creatures need for their physical survival. In addition, the alien monsters taught their 'players' to also participate in their 'Luciferian' rituals, where children are tortured and killed, blood drained, and served as food to all in attendance. You may remember the 'discovered laptop' computer belonging to Representative Weiner; the information of the computer reveals in graphic detail the behavior of top Obama characters, included Hillary Clinton. President Trump has gone after the entire 'pedophile' community, which included many working in the entertainment and music industry. This 'pedophile' community also included many in government service, as well as many in the media and the 'social network' business. Trump will not rest until all of these 'scum' are arrested and sent to prison."

"Yes, I did hear about all of this," Rami announced. "But I was not sure whether all of that was real of just 'fake news'."

"It is very real." "Q" replied. "As of this moment, the following 'big names' who have been indicted include 'former' President George H.W. Bush, who was executed by a military tribunal. His son, George Bush, was also indicted and will soon be executed by the same military tribunals located at the Gitmo U.S. Base in Cuba."

"Are you suggesting that two former American Presidents were arrested and found guilty of 'capital offenses'?" Sheryl asked. "What were their crimes?"

"Both were indicted for their involvement in the death of my father, John F. Kennedy, as well as the attempted assassination of Ronald Reagan." "Q" explained. Those facts are exactly what brought about the attempt on my own life a few years ago, as we discussed earlier."

"Alright" "Q" replied. "let's get back to business."

"OK, we were talking about the 'bad actors' in our government." Caroline explained. "let me give the names of a few other criminals who worked for our government. We identified two former Presidents who were indicted, but there will be at least two other American Presidents who will be indicted. Also, indictments are forthcoming for those involved in the 'Uranium One' deal, as well as the 'Clinton Foundation' problems. Further, as of this date, there have been eighteen (18) attempted assassinations of President Trump. Our organization always knows in advance when these attempts are going to arise, and to date, the President has survived each attempt."

"My God," Rami adds. "The Democrats want him dead this badly?"

"Most of these attempts come from the 'cabal' itself." Caroline replied. "But there are a number of Democrats who have also been involved. All of those involved will be indicted, and in a short time, more than eighty (80) members of the Senate and House will be indicted, mostly Democratic members. But the 'cabal's' reach also includes Republicans. In addition to the Bush family, indictments will reach people like Chaney, John McCain (executed for treason), Vice President Pence (trafficking), Donald Rumsfield, Romney (offshore taxes)."

"You do remember the eight-year Presidency of Obama. A lot of strange things occurred, including the 'Uranium One' deal, as well as Obama's Iran settlement deal. Caroline continued. "The military was not very happy with the behavior of the Administration during the Obama years. It was during this time that ISIS grew from a small 'J.V. Team' into a very power and wealthy terrorist group, taking authority over vast areas in Iraq as well as Syria. The Administration also cut funding to the Military to dangerous levels, which eventually brought the military leadership to consider intervening to stop the direction and future safety of the United States."

"When you say 'intervention'," Sheryl asked "are you talking about a possible 'coup' of the American government?"

"Yes," "Q" replied. "In fact, a small group of military intelligence officers decided that they had no other choice but to remove Obama from his position. This group formed a committee which is today call the "Q" group. I am a part of that group."

"But I assume that your group did not seriously consider 'coup-d-tat'", Sheryl asked. "Please tell me that such an idea did not take effect?"

"No," "Q" replied. "Instead, the ten of us on the "Q" committee decided to see if we could locate a candidate who could actually win the election against the presumed Democratic candidate, Hillary Clinton. We created a list to ten people, took a vote, which narrowed the list to two people, Donald Trump and Ted Cruz. We first approached Trump, who immediately agreed to run for President. Trumps only question was as follows: if elected, do I have to 'do what you ask'? We replied, 'No, just do what you think is right. That is all we ask'."

II. QANON UNLOCKED- SECRETS FROM THE SOURCE

"So, did you engineer the election of 'Trump'? Rami asked.

"Yes, we did." "Q" answered. "You see, the previous Presidential elections were not really 'free elections'. The 'deep state' had control of a 'quantum computer' which was located underneath the Denver airport. Each election, going all the way back to the Bush/Gore Presidential election, was controlled by the 'quantum computer' controlled by the 'deep state'. In fact, the 'deep state' elected George H.W. Bush, Bill Clinton, George Bush, Hussein Obama and were prepared to elect Hillary Clinton in 2016."

"So how did your organization disable the 'quantum computer'?" Sheryl asked.

"We used their own trick against them." "Q" announced. "We took away their computer's abilities half-way through the night of the election, and then used our own 'quantum computer' to insure the election of Donald Trump. So, when we say that Donald Trust was 'selected', and not 'elected', we mean what we say!"

"I do not believe what you are saying?" Sheryl added. "Are you certain of what you say?"

"This is God's truth." Caroline replied. "We just did to the 'deep state' what they had been doing to American over the last twenty-eight years."

"Oh My God!" Sheryl cried out. "I do not know what to say"

"We did what was necessary to save not only this world, but to save the entire world." Caroline replied. "We are working on three major problems in this world: the alien problem, the 'cabal/pedophile' problem, the 'banking problem, and the problem involving 'free elections' in the U.S.A."

7
DONALD TRUMP - WILD CARD

Now we come to December 23, 2016, the date on which President Obama signed into law the updated National Defense Authorization Act.

Aside from funding the military and extending the provision that allows for arrest and incarceration without trial of anyone "suspected" of being associated with terrorism, something else was added but buried deep inside the legislation - the "Countering Disinformation and Propaganda Act."

The irony of this is that the US has for many decades engaged in its own form of disinformation and propaganda, both domestically and internationally, through outlets such as Voice of America, National Public Radio, the New York Times, the Washington Post and most if not all of the mainstream (fake stream) media.

It is another sign that the "gray men" are doing everything they possibly can to hold on to the reins of power - even though those reins are slipping through their fingers at an accelerating pace.

There is a policy in the establishment media of not reporting the many assassination threats that are made against the president, although they do mention the occasional event when it suits their agenda - their agenda being, in the case of Donald Trump, character assassination.

II. QANON UNLOCKED- SECRETS FROM THE SOURCE

Independent assessments have shown that since Donald Trump's election, the mainstream media coverage has been up to 97 per cent negative.

That's why the mainstream media front has been filled with a constant barrage of fake news about Russia having hacked into the Democratic National Committee files and released emails to Wikileaks, which in turn supposedly released them on the Internet, which in turn (the mainstream media would have us believe) influenced the election campaign in favor of Donald Trump.

There's another way to look at this though, and that is, instead of seeing a conspiracy involving Russia and the Trump campaign, how about a conspiracy involving puppets of the gray men within both parties, in all of the US intelligence agencies, and the mainstream media - a conspiracy to discredit or obstruct the new president in every possible way.

You may recall the media reports that Trump was briefed by intelligence agencies which expressed what they called "a high degree of confidence" that Russia did what they say Russia did. And yet, they have also admitted that there is no way to say exactly how Russia's "interference" actually affected the election results.

Nor did they offer any specific proof at all that Russia was responsible for any hacking. They just claimed to have "a high degree of confidence," which really means nothing at all without facts and real evidence to back it up.

It was all a deliberate ploy.

With the puppet media and puppet journalists staying focused on the "Russia did it" meme, along with their "everyone else is fake news" claims - while they themselves propagate all the fake news they can make up about Russia - anything to do with the revelations in those emails about the Clinton Foundation or Clinton Charities or about an active pedophile and child-trafficking ring and other horrendous activities is effectively off the radar.

Such is the art of perception management by politicians, bureaucrats and the media.

MR. BABYLON

They want us all to hate the president, and they're doing it using one of their assassination techniques. It's called character assassination.

Instead of getting sucked into their agenda, shouldn't we be thinking for ourselves, and asking ourselves, just who is this new president?

Before we get to a prophecy Ramtha made about President Donald Trump meeting UFOs, it would be prudent to look at the background of this man who is now the 45th president of the United States.

Now that he has shocked the gray men to the core by winning the election despite all the negative publicity, the manipulation of voting in the primaries, and the regular character assassination "leaks" that occurred, the new president is in the White House, and it looks like he's determined to stay.

As for his background, here's a shorthand version gleaned from the public record.

COURT CASES AND BANKRUPTCIES

Around 500 bodies of evidence against Trump were excused. He won multiple times, lost 38 - and the consequences of the rest are hazy to the extent the open record goes.

While his rivals have intentionally suggested that Trump has been a bankrupt, he has never by and by petitioned for financial protection. Or maybe, his lodging and club organizations have been pronounced bankrupt multiple times, however that was done intentionally so as to rearrange obligation with banks and proprietors of stock and bonds.

RUN FOR THE WHITE HOUSE

Over the years, Mr. Trump considered running for various political offices, but it wasn't until June 16, 2015, two days after his 69th birthday, by which time he was worth over $4 billion, that he announced his candidacy for the 2016 presidential election.

II. QANON UNLOCKED - SECRETS FROM THE SOURCE

Trump paid much of the expenses of his campaign from his own fortune, and he now donates his presidential salary to various causes. He works as president for $1 a year.

HARD TIMES AND DIRTY TRICKS

The New York Times, which throughout the campaign was clearly biased against Trump.

Dirty tricks from a biased media have always been part of the election process, but the same goes for politicians themselves - they resort to every underhanded trick they can think of in their efforts to win votes

Project Veritas, which produced a series of short election-related YouTube videos using under-cover methods, revealed that Clinton campaign insiders were deliberately setting up confrontational protests, including the use of clowns, and planning to bus Democrat voter's interstate to boost her vote and poll numbers.

Although they would deny that they had any intention of influencing voters, publications like Politico, The Washington Post, The New York Times, and the Los Angeles Times all took pleasure in running anti-Trump articles. All of them would claim they were simply pointing out what they termed as lies or falsehoods in Trump's campaign statements.

If that was true of Trump, it was equally true of the Clintons.

A record 84 million people watched the first debate between Donald Trump and Hillary Clinton, after which Trump's opponents went into overdrive, leaking a tape of Trump making lewd comments about women - for which he later apologized.

Trump responded in one of the next debates by telling an inconvenient truth - that Bill Clinton had not just made lewd comments about women. Trump said Bill Clinton had actually 'abused women' and that Hillary had "bullied her husband's victims."

Bill Clinton, he said, "was impeached and lost his license to practice law and paid an $850,000 fine to one of the women, Paula Jones."

Those who wish to split hairs, as attorneys and some journalists tend to do, point out that the $850,000 was not a fine, as Trump claimed, but a settlement, without Bill Clinton admitting liability as to the charge - which was one of harassment in that he (Clinton) had exposed himself to Jones in a hotel room in 1991.

The way the US electoral system is set up, the final decision on who gets to be president is made by what's known as the Electoral College. While Hillary Clinton won the popular vote (and there are questions about whether that was achieved by devious means), Trump won the decisive Electoral College vote.

That was an absolute shock to the Globalists who had done everything they could to ensure that Hillary Clinton would be elected.

Nevertheless, she and her political machine were not about to go quietly. Instead, they were planning every conceivable way to discredit and destroy the man who had thrown a monkey wrench into their Globalist plans.

That was when the Democrats and their allies in high places came up with the "Russia Interfered" and "Russia and Trump" smear campaign.

SMEAR BY SMUT

Something very strange happened just prior to the inauguration, and here again we may sense the presence of the gray men and their puppets. In early January, Trump was briefed by top intelligence agency officials, including the then head of the CIA, on allegations that Russia had "potentially compromising personal and financial information" about him.

A private intelligence dossier was later leaked to the media and to the public containing the claims. Some of the material alleged dubious sexual and financial conduct by Trump, and reporter Bob Woodward called the unsubstantiated dossier a "garbage document" meriting an apology from whoever wrote and leaked it.

Keep in mind that character assassination is one of the tools of politicians everywhere, but it has proven particularly useful in the past for the Globalist/New World Order people who have been very careful about putting their own followers into positions of power, and not just as politicians, prime ministers or presidents. Many of them are the people who make up The Deep State, being in positions of power within various government departments where they usually have long-term tenure.

Many of them can be found within the media and government agencies, especially the intelligence community.

Leaking that totally unsubstantiated document with all its salacious lies and the ensuing media frenzy no doubt harmed Trump's image in the eyes and minds of many, which it was intended to do.

And then came the inauguration.

But first, let's look at two incidents involving President Trump and UFOs.

8
SYMBOLISMS

This title and statement first appeared in Q post #184, repeated to some degree in several later posts (i.e., Q post #1002 "Symbolism will be their downfall."), and refers to the use of both historically occult and "domestic" symbols by Elite members of political groups, religious and scientific organizations, financial and academic institutions, and even powerful royal families. Specifically mentioned in post #184 are the icons of the "owl" and the letter "Y", although quite different in literal appearance, they do connect in occult ways not readily perceived. However, symbolism in general and even in regards to these Elite - often at the center of conspiratorial global agendas - is not limited to these two listed here and as such I will outline three categories of symbols one might encounter when reading the Q drops.

Symbols, most often represented throughout history as (but certainly not limited to) geometric patterns, usually in conjunction with numerical or mathematical significance, are used for a variety of purposes. They may be used as "identifiers" to signal like-minded individuals or to communicate ideas and concepts when words alone cannot. On occasion, symbols used in a magickal or ritual setting can be utilized in a way that heightens the emotions and focuses the intent of the practitioner. (As a side note, magick or magickal is purposefully spelled with a "k" in order to differentiate from regular stage magic. This alteration of the word is commonly

II. QANON UNLOCKED - SECRETS FROM THE SOURCE

attributed to the infamous early 20th century occultist Aliester Crowley but is widely used by many people for the same reason given.) These types of symbols, such as the "Y" mentioned in the Q post above, range from the simply positioned (though quite complex in its philosophical and spiritual implications) Christian cross to the elaborately designed sigils of the Keys of Solomon - see and compare the images shown below:

One may also encounter symbols of a "physical" nature or of a seemingly mundane characteristic, but even so, this does not reduce the power or meaning of the symbol. For the sake of simplicity and to appeal to the understanding of those unfamiliar with such concepts, I will use the widely known mythological Bible tale of Adam and Eve as an example. (Another side note - myths are often regarded as "fictional" accounts or just silly stories that our ancestors told to explain why the sun comes up, but in fact are deep narratives which convey a greater truth about ourselves.) In this story, Eve is tempted by the snake to eat the "apple" or fruit from the Tree of Knowledge. The apple here is the physical or mundane object and is symbolic of the concept of the Knowledge of Good and Evil, which in itself is a symbolic aspect of the Tree. This action of consuming the apple of course leads to the ousting of Adam and Eve from the Garden of Eden. (see figure below)

While the apple is a very general and generic example of "physical object" occult symbolism, there remains a "domestic" or "contemporary" subcategory of this type. Without exploring this subject in great detail, as there are numerous other resources for those interested, an excellent example (although quite malevolent in implication according to released law enforcement memos) would be the coded imagery of pizza originally gleaned from certain leaked emails and pertaining to a certain unnamed restaurant. Pizza is a "domestic" type of symbolism as it has only existed in relatively modern times and is encountered by the population on an everyday "mundane" manner. However, this "pizza" example can also be represented by the type of geometrical patterns previously described, and are not limited to a modern interpretation. The first image below is a direct correlation that one can make between the implied meanings of "pizza" and this geometric representation put out by law enforcement.

Alternatively, while not exactly the same, similar images have appeared throughout history and have held different meanings not necessarily attributed to the dark and perverse context as some people have implied in relation to the previously mentioned emails. For example, we can see a relation with this triangular spiral image with the valknut of Norse origin and the god Odin.

This symbol of three interlocking triangles was, according to Ellis Davidson in the book Gods and Myths of Northern Europe,

One could speculate, although loosely and probably falsely, that the "binding" power and meaning was carried forward (either intentionally or unintentionally) and applied to the modern pizza-spiral symbol without having any direct relation to Norse mythology. I will state here that it is not my belief or intention to promote any real connection between the ancient and modern symbols, only to point out that (just like information) symbols are not in and of themselves positive or negative. It is only until placed within an individual's framework of intention do, they take on one or more of those perceived qualities. A skull-and-crossbones image can have a negative impact as pirates (or a secret society) attempt to loot and kill their targets or it can have a resulting positive result appearing on a bottle of poison, preventing someone from drinking the toxic substance and saving their life.

Third, and lastly, of the symbolic categories covered here are those of archetypes. Primarily attributed to depth-psychologist Carl Jung for originally coining the term, archetypes are often the most complex of symbols as they encompass multiple levels of meaning, appearance, and description mostly in relation to the human psyche. They not only manifest as characters in stories and myths but they quite often appear in more subtle areas like dreams. Many archetypes have qualities that tend to hit a "primal nerve" and the concepts that are related to them can be felt regardless of one's culture, creed, location, or generation in which they lived. However, one can also experience personal archetypes aside from or in addition to those existing in humanity's mass subconscious mind.

Let us again examine the previous mythological example of the story of Adam and Eve, although I am only translating this in the most elementary way in hoping that readers can begin with at least the most accessible understanding. In this story appears the third character of the serpent, which is perhaps one of the most ancient and long-standing archetypes among the human race. (see figure below)

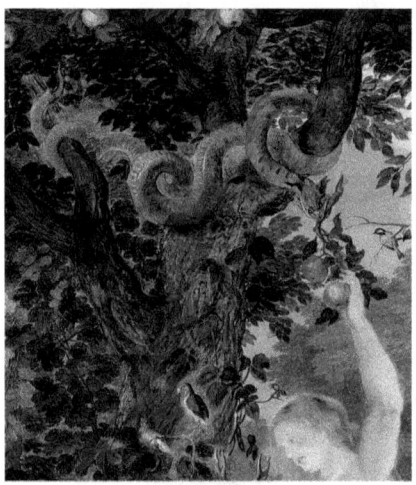

Throughout history and across the globe, the image of the snake or serpent has held many meanings but quite often, as seen in the Garden of Eden story as the animal symbol of Satan or Lucifer, those in Western cultures have a deep underlying notion of aversion, fear, or even revilement without even consciously thinking about it. Part of this, as I tend to think, is merely because of our cultural programming and thus becomes evident in our encounters with real physical snakes. The other part of this reaction, though, seems in some way inherent of genetic or ancestral memory and thus is actually a natural reaction for people even without exposure to theological belief systems. In contrast to this, there are

II. QANON UNLOCKED - SECRETS FROM THE SOURCE

images of the serpent which represent entirely alternate meanings. From the Egyptians and Greeks comes the symbol (and, according to psychologist Carl Jung, who coined the archetype term) of the Ourobouros - a cosmic serpent eating its own tail relaying the cycles of existence - later adopted by alchemists and magicians. (see figure below)

While there is nothing overtly sinister about the symbolism of this serpent, one can imagine or pull from one's subconscious a possible feeling of fear in relation to the contemplation of one's own mortality. It could also be fear of the unknown, fear of self-destruction, or any number of other negative attributes that one could imply. In this way, the possibility exists to link one symbolic representation to another (i.e., the Serpent of Eden) with an underlying psychological effect while having no actual significant contextual connection. This is the primary function of the archetype as symbol.

Please take a moment to remember the "owl" mentioned in Q post #184. The owl is, for many, aside from its form being a traditional cultural symbol, also an archetype in its own right. (See image below)

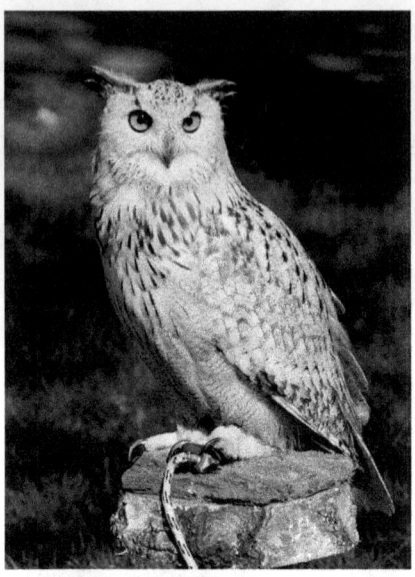

The owl can embody so much and can personally contain so much meaning that it would be impossible to devote even several books about it. Although Q is most likely referencing here a certain statue of an ancient god and an Elite ritual called the Cremation of Care, (see image below)

I suggest that the reader think deeply about the context of owl symbolism in one's own life and what it means in contrast to Q's post. If the reader feels adventurous on this specific archetype (from a QAnon 40,000 ft. advantage), I would suggest investigating a book called The Messengers:

II. QANON UNLOCKED- SECRETS FROM THE SOURCE

Owls, Synchronicity and the UFO Abductee by Mike Clelland although this has no correlation to QAnon - merely an interesting rabbit hole which to travel down.

The mention of the owl in Q post #184, as previously mentioned, also has a strictly aesthetic connection to the "Y" as an incarnation of the ancient god Moloch only in an implied way: The symbol of "Y" is representative of the "bull" or "horned oxen" characteristics of Moloch and is mentioned in the Bible numerous times (as well as other sources like John Milton's Paradise Lost) and has a deep association with the act of child sacrifice, often associated with some of the rituals allegedly performed by members of politically powerful secret societies. This is how we connect the deity of Moloch to the statue of the owl, though no religious or historical evidence exists. Moloch imagery is also manifested in the symbolism of the Minotaur from Greek mythology as the creature who dwelt in the Labyrinth and feasted upon humans. I shall explore this specific tangent at a later point in the book.

There are other categories of symbols such as omens, but from my viewpoint they are not directly relative to the QAnon information drops, whilst also remembering that the three of which I have mention are mainly conveyed by Q through written text on the internet. Mythology, as a whole, incorporates iterations of all types of symbolism in story form. By becoming properly acquainted with how symbolism can potentially impact an individual and the framework in which symbols might appear, one can gain a degree of insight into the subliminal motives, activities, or beliefs of public figures and groups being scrutinized. Through the use of symbols one can also attain a deeper understanding for the gain of one's own knowledge and understanding or to see things from a different angle that may be more beneficial for a given purpose. In light of the three categories all symbolism (and the deep contemplation of them) give the reader a wider outlook when digging for information and how to apply it. I will not be fully analyzing the entire QAnon posts referenced, and instead leave it to the reader to try for themselves. Don't forget - "Expand your thinking" and "question everything" and you just might discover something that brings your mind closer to a state of freedom.

9
MORE ON SYMBOLISM

In late 2014, Apple, Inc. became the first company to be valued at over $700 billion, making it the most valuable company in the history of mankind. And their logo just happens to be a single image that corrals and encompasses exactly the Great Plan? Of mankind seeking knowledge (technology) along the path to becoming an immortal?

Pardon the pun, but was Apple picked to be one of the torchbearers for the Great Plan of advancing man's technological capabilities? Or were they marked for success because they were inviting in otherworldly help with their occult symbol?

Whether the founders of Apple intended it or not, Satan and his demonic host are attracted to symbols that can call upon and welcome their interference in our world. This is exactly why symbols are used in Satanic ceremonies, such as the pentagram and hexagram. They are virtually a 'seal of approval' from the humans that the evil ones have our permission to come and interact with whoever is presenting those symbols.

By Apple, Inc. using the particular symbol they did, they arguably attracted the attention of Satan himself to take that company with that exact logo for the Great Plan and advance them to the top, which is exactly what happened.

How about the #2 most valuable company in the history of mankind, Exxon.

'Exxon' the name contains the symbol of Satan himself in it as you will soon see here. Another coincidence? How about Microsoft? Do you see that Internet Explorer logo on your screen? The one that is a representation of Saturn once you fill in all the blue on the 'e'? Occult symbology is all over the biggest corporations in the world and it's exactly because they are trying to enlist the help of the supernatural.

Symbols are all around us all the time no matter where we are, and they certainly get our attention. Symbols give direction to those who know what they represent. The occult symbols we're going to go over are more than just shapes to be sure. They originated in mankind's ancient history and give directions to the operatives of the New World Order.

I had reservations about sharing with you what we're going to go over because you're never going to be able to look around you the same way ever again, especially the symbol of the Christian cross. The cross is the globally-accepted symbol for Christianity to those who don't know what it really represents.

Unfortunately, the symbol of the cross not only originated in the occult, but it originated as exactly a Satanic symbol. Just like the holidays are truly Satanic, paying homage to the Antichrist King Nimrod and by default Satan, the cross is originally a symbol for Nimrod and Nimrod-reborn on December 25 as Tammuz. The cross was originally called a Tau, named after Tammuz. In ancient Babylon. Just because people believe it represents Jesus does not make it so any more than believing that Christmas is really about Jesus and not the Antichrist. This all goes back to what Jesus told us about loving God with our minds, not our eyes. This is exactly why God forbids any images of anything Divine in the Ten Commandments.

We have been under a constant deception ever since we got here on Earth around 4000 BC, and very, very few have been able to see through this deception, understand it, and warn others exactly what is going on. This is precisely what the prophets did for God back in the day. That's what the Bible is: God's 'called' people telling His followers exactly what's going on, even if it's bad news they just don't want to hear or abide by, let alone accept as bare-bones truth.

How many times did God's prophets call out the ancient Israelis and Judahites for straying, calling them 'a rebellious people'? It seems, as a whole, they were on the naughty list more often than not in the Bible. They were only rebellious in God's eyes though, as all the societies around them had been mired in the Satanic Matrix forever, and they were just joining the crowd basically. When the ancient Israelis strayed, it was just over to the side of 'general society' at the time.

It seems that most of our fellow brethren are in this exact spot today: Following the Satanic holidays, displaying the Satanic symbols, worshipping on Satanically-designated days, chasing money, fame, power. etc. Most of the brethren seem to only step out of the Satanic Matrix for one hour, one day a week……..and it's on the wrong day.

Now, the only way the Great Plan can work is if a small, secretive group of people are controlling it. Not everybody can be the boss on this planet; you need bosses who give direction and workers who execute it. In today's world, the Illuminati are happy to assume the boss role, but they have to prove they are worthy to Satan himself and that's where the occult symbols and ceremonies come in.

When the Great Plan got up and running again in ancient Sumer after the Flood, the proponents of the Great Plan needed occult symbols in order to network. These ancient symbols meant different things to different people. The meanings of the symbols were different to the occultists as opposed to the general population. Satan's people understood the exoteric meaning and the esoteric meaning, but the public-at-large were only meant to understand the exoteric meaning, which is whatever they were told it meant at the time. The exoteric meaning changes from empire to empire, but the original esoteric meaning never changes. This is why they recycle the same symbols over and over. The meaning only changes for the deceived, never for the deceivers.

This is why today people are calling the 'Star of Rephan/Saturn' the 'Star of David'. Most people have no idea the hexagram is representative of Satan himself.

II. QANON UNLOCKED - SECRETS FROM THE SOURCE

Symbols are hugely important to the people running the Great Plan. They didn't have smart phones back then, so they needed to be able to communicate with each other secretly but have their message out where other occultists could see it and know that whatever it was attached to was part of the plan, the Great Plan.

Well my friend, there's not really a 'correct' order to what we're going to go over, other than I tried to categorize the occult symbolism world the best I could. Truly the only way to be considered an 'expert' on the symbolism we're going to go over is to be an insider to the operations of the Illuminati, which I am obviously not.

I think I did a well enough job to get you at least pointed in the right direction. There is such a vast body of information about the New World Order it can be overwhelming and it was before I got saved and everything came into focus. We're just beginning to ramp up a supernatural battle of Biblical proportions and most people don't know the magnitude of what's happening and what's coming just yet, but you certainly do and will know even more as we go forward together in my works.

It is possible that there are even more meanings for the symbols we're going to check, or maybe a debate about my interpretation of one or more. All of it. Anything at all. I welcome open discussion about anything and everything I'm talking about. We're all adults here, this certainly isn't a kid's book. There is nothing in this book people should be afraid to talk about because it's all based on the truthful facts as always.

God wants the people who actively seek it to know the truth about the very things we're talking about, and that is why you are here with me right now, at this point, in this book:

You seek the truth.

SACRED GEOMETRY

Sacred geometry is all around us, all the time. These are the geometric shapes and patterns that our 3D world is constructed of. The very reason geometry is 'sacred' to the occultists is that these shapes and assemblies of shapes originated from the Divine blueprint of how our world operates.

MR. BABYLON

Sacred geometry is found everywhere in our existence, from going from a thought to physical form as a bee makes a honeycomb from perfect hexagons, from a snowflake which always manifests as a hexagonal/6-sided shape, all the way to the very building blocks of life at the subatomic level, which again are typically 6-sided in shape.

The ancients have left us a plethora of evidence that those running the New World Order way back then knew of sacred geometry and put it in designs on everything, from symbols such as the Seed/Fruit/Tree of life to the symbols of the pentagram, hexagram, etc. that are used in black magic/occult rituals.

Not only did the ancient occultists know things that the general population is just now finding out through advancements in science, but by them being shown how to hack into God's natural system by Satan/Azazel and the Watchers way back in the pre-Flood days, they were and are able to obtain even more occult information, prognosis of the future even in my opinion. It's just like they're hacking into God's computer network, with the ways to do this having been passed down over the millennia by the ever-regenerating proponents of the Great Plan. Those ways are exactly the gruesome Satanic blood and sex rituals they perform in honor of their god, Satan.

Sacred geometry has been incorporated into the designs of religious structures of all walks of life, buildings, towns and even entire cities. One look at the street map of Washington D.C. and it's not hard to see that it's laid out according to the occult and many have already made the case showing that it is in fact laid out incorporating occult sacred geometry. Virtually every significant federal building in Washington DC has a Masonic plaque on it, from Washington Monument to the George Washington Memorial, so this should not be a surprise at all around Capitoline Hill.

Sacred geometry has been turned into religious symbols of all types, appearing on religious structures, art, stained glass, amulets, necklaces, bracelets, rings, clothes, and all the rest of it. In other words, it's everywhere you turn and always has been......just like the followers of Satan.

10
THE NEW WORLD ORDER TIMETABLE

The New World Order of the global elites are preparing for themselves underground cities stocked with food, water, ammunition, medication, and other provisions to survive a future life changing event upon the surface of the earth. These underground military facilities are being built secretly in the United States, Israel, England, Russia, Norway, etc. It has been estimated there are at least 150 underground bases in the USA. A selected elite will be residing in these facilities, during a devastating global catastrophe. The bankers in Frankfurt, Germany are constructing bunker sanctuaries. Elite CEOS are purchasing properties in remote areas of the world away from coastlines. Conspiracy theorists claim they are aggressively promoting their smart green technologies, based on the premise of global warming, leading to a cashless society, a one world government, and a microchipped population. Everyone and everything will be reliant on the electric grid through the use of RFID and biometric technologies. Their UN Agenda 21/ 2030 plan of sustainable development, is an agenda of removing personal liberties, such as private ownership of vehicles, property, and guns, where all must recognize the needs of the collective, not the individual, for the common good for a one world government to be implemented by 2030.

These global elites are an occult secret society known as the Illuminati, or referred to as The New World Order. These thirteen bloodline families are all powerful and influential, their wealth and assets accumulated, more than the combined funds of the world. Their members are the most powerful bankers, financiers, celebrities, politicians, and business people that are exclusive to the Bilderberg Group, and the House of Windsor and the Vatican are also included. Their plan of domination of the world is currently unfolding, as they manipulate the world's economies, markets, fund both sides of the wars, control the mainstream media, and work towards 24/7 surveillance of everyone using the technology of RFID chips, and Biometrics. Their quest is for a one world government, religion, cashless society, and the reduction of the world's population level to a sustainable 500 million people, in a world of slightly over 7 billion.

The global elites hold high level positions in key corporations and institutions. Their decisions are consequential to the fate of every human being, and the civilization of the world. They are devoid of moral or ethical principles, their secrecy is the essence of their power, and never risking disclosure. Their agenda includes distraction, and deception, to maintain control of the masses, for they fear uncontrolled societal chaos, a potential threat to their plans for the human race. They have their contingency plans in place, while the population will be the last to know, and the first to perish, while they believe they will remain protected.

Their secret occultist doctrine teaches that the ancient peoples worshiped gods and deities, that traveled to earth, from a planet star known as Sirius. The Egyptians acknowledged this star, as Anubis, the jackal headed God. A statue of Anubis is displayed at the Denver International Airport, as well as other mysterious paintings, and a time capsule. It is believed by conspiracy theorists that the Denver International Airport is the new headquarters for The New World Order. The pagan religions of Babylon, Egypt, and the Sumerian, were based on myths that described reptilian ancient astronauts that visited earth, and mated with women, being worshiped by mankind as gods and or goddesses.

The elites know the future, know what is coming, and have constructed massive protected underground facilities, to sustain their lives for a considerable amount of time. Their observatories and highly powered telescopes give them unlimited access to astronomical and scientific data that we the public are not privy to. Since they control the mainstream media, they keep any credible information from leaking out, debunk any

II. QANON UNLOCKED- SECRETS FROM THE SOURCE

whistle blowers or truth seekers and promote false propaganda. Due to the numerous Nibiru arrival prediction dates that have been proven false; this only helps them persuade the public to ignore the warnings about Planet X. It is believed that scientists and researchers, have discovered the path of Nibiru, and the discoveries have been suppressed, by mysterious disappearances or death, due to their knowledge of this ultimate cover up deception. They know that this crisis will usher in economic and social upheaval, and have made plans to invoke martial law, and set up Fema detention camps for this purpose. If no danger exists to the earth, then why the need for extensive preparations and a cover up of them?

The NOAA has determined that nearly half the population resides in coastal areas. Our Federal government has covertly moved our national capital resources from Washington, D.C. to Denver, Colorado where it is reported the construction of vast underground facilities now exist there, for the headquarters of the New World Order. In addition, the New York Federal Branch of the Federal Reserve has moved its headquarters to Chicago. Danger zones would be the east and west coastlines of North America, South and central England, and big cities, and low-lying areas. Through the use of geoengineering HAARP weather modification programs, they perpetuate the mass deception concept of global warming. Apparently, planned military operations, such as Operation Indigo Sky fold, spray toxic and biological agents in the atmosphere to cover up any evidence of Nibiru in the sky. Pilots are briefed that it is a strategy exercise to combat greenhouse gases and global warming. They create chemtrails in the sky to prevent any visibility of approaching Planet X, with this black op mission.

According to unnamed sources in military intelligence, our public health officials have been preparing for a cataclysmic disaster. Hospitals are storing large provisional supplies such as gas masks, medicine, and body bags. The government has been stockpiling food, ammunition, medication, and water supplies over a period of years. There have been many drills and contingencies for large scale disasters, and a national emergency alert system available on every cell phone that has been established. FEMA who serves the NWO elite will be in charge of dividing the country into zones, after the catastrophe, and implementing martial law. Silence is another tactic that is used by the global elites, as they control the mainstream media and Hollywood, only what they want reported on, will be told, perpetuating their ideals for public consumption. The Illuminati are ruthless and twisted in their ideology, as they feel the rules do not apply to them, because they have the power to make the rules. In their code, they believe that before their enemy is destroyed, they must have a chance to be forewarned through symbolism or clues, so they can have a fighting chance.

Thus, conspiracy theorists believe they use the Hollywood movies of today to suggest dark futures for the planet, invoking occult images, Egyptian myths and symbols, and global disasters. These promoting interplanetary creators of mankind, such as Star Wars, where humans and aliens co-exist with robots or droids., and space travel between planets is common. The force is portrayed as an energy field representing all living things binding the galaxy together. There is the light force for good, the Jedi, and the dark force for evil, the Sith. In Star Trek, Gene Roddenberry, the creator of the series was a 33rd degree Scottish freemason. One masonic symbol is their pyramid shaped communicators, Spock's masonic V sign, and the United Federation seal of planets is very similar to the United Nations seal today. The movie Stargate in 1994, was a sci-fi adventure that led to a planet with humans that resembled ancient Egyptians who worshiped the god RA, with pyramids and this ancient ruler. Deep Impact premiered in 1998, with the storyline of a comet that threatens the earth, unless it can be destroyed, and only those allowed into shelters will survive. The movie 2012, reveals a plot of world leaders that make secret preparations for the survival of the select elite of society to be sheltered on a gigantic ark, while a series of global catastrophes threaten to annihilate mankind. In the premiere of the movie, The Mummy in 2017, a betrayed Egyptian princess that has been entombed under the desert for thousands of years is unearthed, once she is resurrected, she goes on a monstrous rampage. The NWO use occult imagery, hand signals, and place subliminal messages in videos and songs. Prominent hand signals are the hidden eye, all seeing eye, devil's horns, the pyramid sign, and the V sign. The highest levels of freemasonry are devil worship, and covert Satanic religion. Biblical prophecy links the New World Order to Luciferian Freemasonry, whom are under control of the Antichrist.

11
IMMIGRATION, WITCH HUNTS AND HEALTH CARE

Can we make a better tomorrow, a better future for our children? Of course, we can! The question is not really whether we are able, but whether we are willing. As things stand and look at present the answer to the question of whether we are willing seems to be a resounding "No!". There are simply too many people that are not in the least bit interested in changing, much less learning to understand those with differing views and then accepting them as they are. So many are genuinely afraid that if they allow themselves to accept differences and be tolerant of them that they will somehow be betraying their own beliefs and/or views. They are afraid that if they show compassion and tolerance then things will run amok, as if things aren't bad now with them stubbornly clinging to their intolerance and therefore helping to perpetuate the problems we see today. They seem to fear that showing compassion, trying to be more understanding and display tolerance is equivalent to weakness. Take the very hot topic of immigrants and immigration. People, politicians... even entire states are doing everything in their power to try to run immigrants out of the country and also make it impossible for the ones who stay to gain legal citizenship. If you look at it very carefully, you can see it for what it is. Racism and fear. Racism because all the new laws and legislation are designed specifically to target Hispanics, and in particular Mexicans, without outright saying so (to avoid being seen for what it really is). This country was founded by nothing but immigrants! I hear the term "American" so often used in the sense of a race of people, and often added is that in order to be a "good American", one has to hold some very specific views such as America is the only free country in the world, guns are almost equal in status to the Bible, Christianity is (or should be) the official religion of the State, and English is the only language worth speaking. As the joke goes, if you speak three languages you are trilingual. If you speak two languages you a bilingual but if you can only speak one, you are American.

During a recent televised golf tournament, a family member remarked, "OK, we can leave now. At least I know an American is going to win." It wasn't said with a tone of simple patriotism, but rather with a distinct distaste for any other nationality. But back to the immigration issue. States are passing laws that make it very hard for anyone who doesn't have white skin. These laws, regardless of what their proponents claim, are not aimed at, say, Russians or someone from the U.K. No, they are plainly targeting Mexicans. Do these people not understand that we need these immigrants? After all, with unemployment so high, white people are not flocking to the fields to work all day, every day, in the blazing sun, for very little pay and no benefits whatsoever. It's not just in the fields either. There are many jobs that Mexicans do that white people simply refuse to do because it's too hard, pays too little or they simply see the work as somehow beneath them. If all the immigrants (meaning here Mexicans) left as so many of the "good Americans" want them to this country would be in serious trouble. Food prices would skyrocket because nobody would be willing to work in the fields without far more pay than immigrants receive, nor would they do it without insurance and benefits.

That's just one of the areas this country would be in trouble with. As with my statements about politics and politicians, this is simply fact and there is no need to argue it because it is self-evident. Almost everything we use and purchase would skyrocket in price. Not just food, but let's look at what would happen in the fields. Farmers would be forced to pay at least legal minimum wage (that's right, immigrants don't even get that) and provide safer working environments. Immigrants are exploited because it's easy to do so. They are undocumented so what are they going to do, what government agency are they going to complain to? The people who hire them know this. Please don't misunderstand me, I am not at all saying that immigrants should be exploited, I am simply pointing out the fact that they are. They are exploited and looked down upon. And they make an excellent scapegoat for politicians. Blame all crime on immigrants and you have yet another bogeyman for white Americans to be afraid of. After all, it seems we Americans need "others" to be afraid of and blame all our problems on. We don't like taking responsibility for our problems. So, we have our new witch hunts... Mexicans and Muslims. We want to, as evidenced through our entertainment (films, TV, books), news media and politicians, blame all our problems on "others". Blaming virtually all crime, not to mention our economic problems of our own doing, on immigration is simply too convenient. The same with blaming all the world's problems on Islam and Muslims.

Not long ago it was learned that the FBI had been teaching its agents that mainstream American Muslims were most likely all terrorist sympathizers and that Muhammad was a cult leader and nothing more. That's right, the FBI was actually having a class teaching its agents this load of nonsense. The FBI now claims it has stopped the nonsensical "training", and if they actually have, I'm sure it was because of their being caught in such nonsense and not because of their own moral compass. Now police in Arizona and other places are free to racially profile anyone of Hispanic heritage. With all my pointing out these uncomfortable facts, you may think that I am Hispanic or Muslim (or perhaps both) and therefore have some personal or cultural agenda for pointing these things out, but I am neither. I am simply stating the facts, ugly as they are. I also find it odd that, considering our crumbling infrastructure in this country, we can find and spend billions on perpetual wars but seem utterly incapable of repairing/maintaining bridges and roads. We could go a long way toward easing, if not outright ending, hunger not only in our country but around the globe if we put the money, we spend on killing into feeding. And yes, there are people right here in America who go without adequate food, shelter and medical care for those of you who may not be aware of it. The "American Dream" has become a sad joke. Even for those lucky enough to have jobs right now, our society is set up, seemingly designed, to use people up and then discard them. For example, a person is expected to go to public schooling, graduate and get a job (don't forget getting married and having two children), belong to some church, work at that job sitting in that cubicle (or slaving away in the sun), be placed on anti-depressants, antianxiety pills (and don't forget the cholesterol lowering drugs), have a heart attack anyway, retire (if you live long enough) and then try to have enough money to cover all your prescription drugs, food, medical costs and then if you are still alive, be placed in an "assisted living" facility and then finally die. Does that really sound like your idea of a "dream"? To me it sounds like a nightmare! I suggest researching, or better yet (for anyone who can afford it these days) France and the lifestyle of the French or those of other developed European countries. Here is a short list of some of the things European visitors to America notice right away:

Not as many people walk or use bicycles

Everyone looks tired

How big everything is, particularly vehicles (as one noted, "SUVs everywhere!")

Everyone is in a hurry (I'd like to address this one further later)

All the disposable things, particularly cups and silverware (ties in with the above)

Places are always open, and therefore people are always working (also ties in with above)

Notice of the level of consumerism that simply isn't present in their home country

Nobody takes time to enjoy family or life itself

Taking a look at the above things that visitors from Europe several things become apparent but a couple of things become glaringly unmistakable. So, the people all look tired... that's probably got something to do with the fact that everyone is stressed out, over-worked and, as observed, in a hurry. We eat our meals on the go, we are such a people of consumerism and instant gratification that many businesses remain open 24/7, therefore having people working hours far removed from our natural circadian rhythm. We drive vehicles that consume far and away more gasoline/diesel and oil than necessary to get us where we are going. Motorcycles aren't even what you could call mainstream, nor do they fit the typical view of the "American Dream" even though they are a much more fuel-efficient means of transportation. No, you can't take your kids to school on a motorcycle but you can sure commute back and forth to work on one. On the noticing of all the disposable items, particularly cups, forks and knives, we throw almost everything away. I realize this isn't the point the visitors were making. They were making the point that people here rarely sit down and enjoy a meal, instead they take it with them or wolf it down far too fast. My point on the observation of disposable items though is that we use something and then throw it away. We even have disposable phones! Some people trade their overly-large vehicle in for yet another overly-large one every year or two. We simply use, not enjoy. Lastly, they notice that family time and simply stopping to enjoy life is not a very high priority here in America. Even if you never visit a European country, at least take the time to research it via Internet, books or documentary and one thing will become crystal clear very quickly... people there simply don't live their lives at the break-neck speed we do here. They know how to enjoy the things that matter. I'm not trying to make them out to be some sort of Utopian society, because there is no such thing. But I do believe they live a better quality of life and definitely enjoy life on a much larger scale that most Americans do. How many old American CEOs do you know of? If you know of any, how healthy are they? How healthy (mentally as well as physically) is any CEO? How's their family life (if they even have one to speak of)?

12
HOSTILE MIND TAKEOVER

Brainwashing – a scary word. No one wants to believe that they could be brainwashed, but it happens. It happens more than you even know.

Brainwashing is known by other names too – mind abuse, coercive persuasion, and thought control. What happens, is a person or even a group of people use systematic methods to get the victim to bend or conform to things they wouldn't conform to otherwise. Think about members of a cult.

That's scary, but even scarier is the fact that advertisers have learned these dark techniques and use them regularly on the unsuspecting public.

ONLY ONE CONCLUSION

The day was long, the food supply limited, and picky eaters would prove hard to deal with. I was alone with my two sons in a remote cabin in the woods. Their father had gone out hunting and wouldn't be back for at least two days.

We were on our own with the little we had. My ten and twelve-year-old sons didn't care for much, other than fast food. I had my work cut out for me.

II. QANON UNLOCKED - SECRETS FROM THE SOURCE

But how to get pre-teens to think they actually wanted to eat something they'd turned down most of their lives?

"Hey, I was reading the other day how the turkey is a superfood." I brought up.

"Turkey?" Garrett asked as he made a face. My twelve-year-old thought himself a connoisseur of not so fine foods. "If that's such a superfood, then why isn't it sold at any of the places we eat, Mom?"

"Well, grapes are a superfood and you can't get them at the places you eat either." I felt that needed to be pointed out. "And we are out here in the wilderness - twenty miles from any town. If your dad doesn't make it back for any reason, then we'll have to hoof it out of here. And the snow is only getting deeper by the day."

"Are you saying that we should build ourselves up in case we have to walk out of here, Mom?" Bryan, our ten-year-old asked.

I shrugged. "You never know. Might as well be prepared, right?"

My sons looked at each other than Garrett asked, "So, what about this turkey you read about?"

"It's a superfood. It's got protein and other vital nutrients."

"Yeah, and it's gross," Bryan said.

"Do you think that muscle building protein is gross, Bryan?" I asked.

Garret flexed his tiny bicep. "I'm strong enough."

"Are you?" I looked out the window as the snow fell outside of it. "Are you strong enough to fend off, let's say, a wolfpack?"

Both boys looked a little on the frightened side. "Nope," they said.

"Do you think that eating a superfood, like a turkey could help you fight them off if it came to it?" I asked.

Bryan nodded. "Superfood is in the name, so I would think it could help."

"And what about hunger? Walking all that way, twenty miles could deplete your energy. My bets are on that it would. Wouldn't it be best to have fueled your body with the best stuff you could so that you would have stamina much longer than if you'd eaten junk?"

Garret agreed, "Yeah, eating superfoods sounds like the best thing to do if you're faced with something like that."

"Yeah," Bryan agreed.

"So, if you had the choice to eat cheese pizza or a turkey sandwich on whole grain bread, which would you pick if you had to walk twenty miles in the snow and possibly take on a pack of wolves along the way?"

"Turkey sandwiches!" they both shouted.

"Great." I got up to go make them some. "Since we have no idea what we're in for. Do you boys think tonight's dinner should be some turkey sandwiches or that one frozen cheese pizza we've got?"

"Turkey sandwiches!" they shouted again.

And we have a winner!

THE SAME PHRASE

"My mother had a new friend over the other day and something she said just won't leave my mind," I told my husband. "And Mom has been going to meet with this little church group with this woman for over a week. Now, Mom's saying this thing a lot and I don't know if I like it."

"What is it?" he asked me.

"It seems benign. I know it does, but it's just that her friend said it over and over. And now Mom's doing it." I couldn't shake the feeling that something bad might happen if I didn't tell someone what I'd overheard.

"So, what is it, Beth?" my husband asked, growing impatient.

"The name of the man who heads up this little church group – a group who meets in the member's homes, instead of a real church – is Barney." Even saying his name gave me chills.

II. QANON UNLOCKED- SECRETS FROM THE SOURCE

"And what does that have to do with what this woman and your mother have been saying?" he asked me, looking aggravated as he rubbed his temples.

"It's his name. The woman kept starting out her sentences with, Barney says. It was odd. She said things like Barney says we should all eat tuna fish. My mother asked her why and I swear to you that the woman merely shrugged and said that she didn't know. No one asks Barney why he says the things he says – that would be rude. Anyway, she went on to say that since she's added tuna to her diet, she feels great."

"That's not so bad," my husband said as he laid back in our bed. "I don't see what you're worried about."

"She said other things too. Like this, Barney said we all need to put ten dollars into the pot each time we meet. And she also said Barney, says we need to meet every other day, so we don't forget the words." I shrugged. "I don't know what she meant by that, but I didn't like it. And I didn't like what I found at Mom's today."

"What did you find at your mother's house?"

"A whole shelf in her pantry is nothing but canned tuna fish. And she's got an envelope from her bank with nothing but ten-dollar bills in it too." I just knew something wasn't right with this little church group. "And she told me that she joined that group and then she said this, Barney says we should all bring at least one new person to our group each month. Barney says when we get one hundred followers that we can buy a place where we all can live. Like a camp. We will all live in one, great big home, and we will all take care of each other for the rest of our lives."

"Great!" my husband said. "I've always worried that your mother would end up living out the remainder of her years with us. Thank goodness she found this group."

"No! I think he's a cult leader or something." I smacked him on the arm. "She said that Barney says they are all going to put all their money into one account that he'll oversee and make sure everyone is taken care of."

"I still don't see a downside," my husband said, then snuggled down and went to sleep.

TOO MANY QUESTIONS

"How would you like it if a man took your wallet, Joey?" he asked me.

"I," I couldn't say anything else as he jumped right back in.

"How would you like it if someone stole your dog, Joey? How would you like it if you stepped on a nail? How would you like it if your mom went to jail? How would you like it if I took your stuffed teddy bear? How would you like it if you couldn't ever drink water again?"

"Stop!" I screamed.

But he didn't stop. "How would you like it if popcorn were no longer available? How would you like it if there wasn't any more snow, Joey? How would you like it if I ran over your toe with my car?"

"I wouldn't like any of those things."

"So, how would you like to go to the movies with me?"

"Movies? Yeah, sure." I hadn't wanted to go anywhere with him, but I'd do anything to shut him up.

WHEN FEAR BENDS YOUR MIND

I sat at my desk in my office on the fifth floor when a strange man ran into my office, breathing hard and looking scared to death. "Thank God, I made it." He slammed the door closed behind him, locking it. "There's a fire out there. The whole place is on fire. I'm looking for all the survivors I can find to help them." He came at me quickly, pulling me out of my chair. "You've got to get out of here."

"I don't smell any fire."

"No, it's not quite here yet. But it's coming and it's coming fast. You're going to have to jump."

"I'm on the fifth floor! I can't jump."

"You would rather burn alive?"

"I would not rather burn alive."

He pushed me to the window then opened it. The ground looked so far away. "Here you go then, time to jump."

"But," I got up on the ledge. "I don't see any smoke."

"It's billowing out the other side. Hurry, there's no time to waste." He gave me a slight push. "Jump! Now!"

And so, I did and that was when I broke my legs all because of one crazy as sin man.

ISOLATION AND BRAINWASHING

Joe grew up on a remote farm with only his grandparents around. With only the three of them, Joe knew nothing more than what he'd been told his entire life.

When I got out of the car to pick him up and take him with me to a new home, a place where he'd be safe since the death of his grandparents, he tried to run away. "No. I won't go. You're not real!"

I had another caseworker come in from behind the small house. "It's okay. We're here to help you, Joe."

"No!" the fifteen-year-old boy screamed. "There's no one else on this planet. Why would they lie to me? Why?"

Joe was the victim of grandparents who thought it best to keep the boy unaware of outside life. They'd had to raise him from an infant when his mother took off and left him at their home. She was in a cult and they wouldn't let her keep the baby she'd been pregnant with before she joined them.

I had to try to make him understand why people he loved would do such a horrible thing to him, "They did it only because they loved you, Joe. But it was all a lie. Now come with us and everything will be okay. I promise."

He fell to his knees in the dark dirt. "They promised me too, lady. They promised me too!"

MR. BABYLON

BRAINWASHING IN ADVERTISING

I sat there, my toothbrush in hand and the tube of toothpaste that I'd used for years and years in the other. "Nine out of ten dentists recommend this brand, Danny. You should use it too."

"How do you know that's true?" My new boyfriend came to stand at my side. "I use the other brand and guess what?"

"What?" I asked as I began brushing my teeth.

"That commercial says that nine out of ten dentists recommend my brand too. Think you might've been brainwashed?"

Have I?

13
JOHN F. KENNEDY'S ASSASSINATION

A bit over 50 years ago, President John F. Kennedy was murdered on tour to Dallas, Texas, two years after his term. A Warren Commission inquiry concluded a retired U.S. Navy seal called Lee Harvey Oswald fired Kennedy from a local book depository; however, the unclear nature of the event contributed to a variety of possible hypotheses.

Most theories of JFK center on the notion that Oswald did not operate alone. The convoy was approaching a grassy knoll on the northern side of Elm Street when the president was struck by the bullet that killed him. Newspaper photos show that police captured three tramps hidden in a train car behind knoll soon after the attack. Since the people were found to be clean-shaven and well-fed, rumors emerged that they were agents of the CIA rather than crack heads.

The suggestion that the murder was a CIA scheme seems insane, but theories say the president's supposed statement that he wished to "cut the CIA into a thousand bits and spread it to the winds" has made him an agency priority. Many reports say that one of the hobos was E. Howard Chase, a former CIA agent who was interested in overthrowing Cuban leader Fidel Castro in the poorly-fated Bay of Pigs project.

Another theory is mafia related. But why is it that the mafia wishes JFK dead? Robert, his brother, turned on the pressure on organized crime. At the moment, Robert was the US secretary of state, and his "anti-mafia campaign" has contributed to a dramatic rise in the number of top mafia members arrested.

Another hypothesis claims that JFK was murdered because they demonstrated so considerable interest in "evil practices." There are two "crucial" pieces of evidence to support this. The first one was a letter JFK sent to the CIA asking to see classified UFO files. The other was a notice from a top CIA official stating, "We can't authorize" the president to see all the information confidential.

The underground puppet masters running the planet are easy targets for a conspiracy by JFK. The president wanted to get rid of Illuminati; it was claimed that he tried to stop the Vietnam War, a fight that yielded the lovely dividends of the "shadowy banks." JFK's efforts to "rein in" the influence of the US Treasury department have "affected" the Freemasons, sparking a lethal revolt.

Another theory blames the guy holding the black umbrella. Several sources refer to a "mysterious" individual carrying an umbrella as the motorcade of JFK passed past. The assassination day was nice and bright; no one in the crowd, but one individual, is sporting a raincoat or holding an umbrella. And he was seen exactly where someone fired the bullets.

People who claim that the CIA was responsible for the assassination of Kennedy suspect that the government actively criticized a variety of positions regarding Cuba and socialism. The hypothesis suggests that Jfk's failure to provide air cover for the unsuccessful invasion of Bay of Pigs, a plan supported by the CIA to topple Fidel Castro, prompted the CIA to remove Kennedy completely from the scene.

A similar hypothesis claims that the CIA has been collaborating with the Mob to execute Kennedy. The two groups at the time had a common purpose in overturning Castro because the Mob owned a variety of high-risk stakes in Cuban businesses that were shut down. Some claim that the operation was much less complex than a government coup, albeit undertaken by a group of disgruntled Cuban exiles who saw the attempted invasion of the Bay of Pigs as ample proof that Kennedy was unfit for president.

II. QANON UNLOCKED- SECRETS FROM THE SOURCE

One hypothesis argues that in the 1964 race, Lyndon B. Johnson hated being stripped so deeply from the Presidential ballot that he was planning to have JFK killed.

This is accurate that Kennedy wanted to succeed Johnson as vice-president, according to a 1968 autobiography published by Kennedy's assistant, Evelyn Lincoln. On 19 November 1963, Kennedy told Lincoln as much — three days before he was assassinated. Many historians also claim that an assassination of Kennedy, guided by Premier Nikita Khrushchev, was carried out by a band of Soviet officers.

Ultimately, at the end of the Cuban Missile Crisis of 1962, Khrushchev was compelled to withdraw the nuclear missiles that he had installed in Cuba owing to US military attacks towards the Soviet Union.

Conspiracists say that the change inspired Khrushchev to destroy Kennedys" lobbies had been significantly destroyed prior to the towers' demise. There were no chance the jet's impact caused too extensive destruction 80 floors below.

GLOSSARY

Because Q's posts include terms you may not be familiar with, I've provided a glossary to help decode abbreviations, acronyms, symbols, names, and agencies. The decodes I've provided are not to be taken as the only possible correct ones. There are, no doubt, valid decodes

I have not considered and have not included. Some abbreviations have been confirmed by Q to have multiple meanings. As Q's mission continues, some abbreviations that have been used in one way may later be used in a different way. In such cases, the context of a particular post should be used to determine the best interpretation. The terms in this glossary are not exclusive to posts found in this book. They pertain to the entirety of Q's operation to date.

Note: names and initials are alphabetized as they appear in Q posts which is usually the first name followed by the last name.

/calmbeforethestorm/ or /CBTS/ --- An 8chan board where Q has posted messages.

/greatawakening/ or /GA/ --- A read-only board on 8chan where Q has posted.

/patriotsfight/ or /pf/ --- An 8chan board where Q has posted messages.

GLOSSARY

/pol/ --- Boards on 4chan and 8chan where Q has posted messages.

/projectdcomms/ --- A read-only board on 8kun where Q posts.

/qresearch/ --- Boards on 8chan and 8kun where anons can interact with Q.

/thestorm/ --- An 8chan board where Q has posted messages.

/_ --- A three-sided shape used by Q to illustrate the power structure of the three wealthiest and most politically influential families in the world; the Saudi royal family (removed from power in 2017) the Rothschilds, and George Soros. Q's mission involves the gradual removal of all three sides of the triangle, representing the removal of these families from power.

#FLY# --- Q uses the word FLY along with a name and pound sign (#) to indicate a person whose influence has been neutralized or a politician who has been removed from office.

[ ] --- Brackets indicate different things depending on the context. Q answered an Anon's inquiry by indicating that brackets signified a "kill box" but sometimes brackets are used to highlight letters that spell out a message hidden within a post, for example, [p], [r], [a], [y]. Brackets can also be used to disrupt computer programs used by opponents that search Q's posts for key words.

[F] --- Foreign

(You) --- When viewing posts on 4chan, 8chan, or 8kun, the word "you" is displayed in parenthesis to indicate that you are viewing your own post.

4-10-20 --- Initials of Donald John Trump when the numbers are replaced with the corresponding letters of the alphabet.

4chan --- An internet message board where users can post anonymously.

5 Eyes or Five Eyes or FVEY --- A multilateral intelligence-sharing alliance that includes Australia, Canada, New Zealand, the United Kingdom and the United States.

7 Dwarves --- According to the Michael Kilian article Spy vs. Spy published in 2000 by The Chicago Tribune, the CIA has seven supercom-

GLOSSARY

puters named after the seven dwarves; Doc, Dopey, Bashful, Grumpy, Sneezy, Sleepy and Happy.

5:5 --- "Five by five" is military jargon signifying loud and clear, or understood. Radio transmissions are rated for signal clarity and strength on a scale from 1-5 with 1 being the lowest and 5 being the highest. 5:5 indicates the signal is loud and clear.

8chan --- An internet message board where users can post anonymously.

8kun --- An internet message board where users can post anonymously. Created in 2019 after 8chan was de-platformed.

A or A's --- Agency, agencies, intelligence agencies.

Alice and Wonderland --- A signature phrase that Q helped anons decode. Alice is Hillary Clinton. Wonderland is Saudi Arabia. Q says Saudi Arabia has been the source of funding for many U.S. politicians.

Alphabet --- The parent company of Google, YouTube, and others subsidiaries.

Alice --- Hillary Clinton, as she was referred to in emails from Marty Torrey (published by WikiLeaks), who went by the moniker "Hatter."

Bakers --- Slang term for anons who assemble 4chan, 8chan, or 8kun posts (crumbs) into threads (breads) for discussion.

BB --- U.S. Attorney General William (Bill) Barr.

BC --- Bill Clinton, 42nd president of the United States from 1993 to 2001.

CA --- In most cases, it refers to California, but when used in a stringer with Uranium One (U1), it refers to Canada.

C-Info --- Confidential or Classified Information.

C_A --- Central Intelligence Agency, A civilian foreign intelligence service of the U.S. federal government.

CM --- Code Monkey, the administrator who provided technical support for Q's board on 8chan, and the current administrator of 8kun.

GLOSSARY

DJT --- Donald John Trump, the 45th President of the United States. Before entering politics, he was a businessman and television personality.

Eagle --- Secret Service code name for President Bill Clinton.

Epstein Island --- Little Saint James Island, owned by Jeffrey Epstein

Fag --- Slang term for an anon. It is sometimes combined with areas of interest, i.e. biblefag, planefag, lawfag, etc.

Fake wood --- Hollywood

Fantasy Land --- A Q signature indicating a truth that is too wild for the average person to believe. Cognitive dissonance is caused by information that challenges a programmed way of thinking.

Game Theory --- The study of conflict and cooperation by opponents within a competitive game environment.

Gang of 8 --- A term used to describe the eight leaders in the United States Congress who are briefed on classified intelligence matters. It includes the leaders of both parties from the Senate and House of Representatives, and the chairs and ranking minority members of both the Senate and House Intelligence Committees.

GCHQ --- An acronym for the Government Communications Headquarters, an intelligence and security organization responsible for providing signals intelligence (SIGINT) and information to the UK government and armed forces.

Honeypot --- A scheme used to lure people into behaviors that are unethical, immoral, or illegal. Their participation can be recorded and used as leverage to control them.

HRC --- Hillary Clinton, former Secretary of State under Barack Obama. Democratic Presidential Candidate in 2016. Wife of President William Jefferson Clinton.

IRL --- In real life, as opposed to online.

JA --- Julian Assange, founder of WikiLeaks, a watchdog organization that publishes leaked documents.

Marker --- A reference in a post by Q intended to mark a topic.

GLOSSARY

Moar --- Slang term for "more" used on 4chan, 8chan, and 8kun.

Mockingbird --- Operation Mockingbird was a CIA operation where the agency recruited news reporters and their managers to disseminate propaganda for the purpose of controlling the masses.

Mueller --- Robert Mueller, former FBI Director and Special Counsel.

NSA --- National Security Agency is a signals intelligence agency within the U.S. Department of Defense. It collects and analyzes electronic signals intelligence of interest to the security of the U.S. and protects all classified and sensitive information stored on government information technology equipment. In addition, the NSA supports and contributes to the civilian use of cryptography and computer security measures.

NWO --- New World Order, sometimes referred to as a one-world government. A governmental concept where individual nations surrender their political sovereignty to the will of a centralized world governmental power.

Pain or [PAIN] --- A reference to the pending prosecution of corrupt individuals.

PG --- Pizzagate/PedoGate, an internet controversy that surfaced in 2016, where restaurant owner James Alefantis and John Podesta were accused of pedophilia.

Q Clearance --- Access to the highest level of classified information in the U.S. Department of Energy. Q suggested in his case; it refers to the highest level of access across all departments.

R's --- Republicans

RM --- Robert Mueller, Special Counsel who investigated President Donald Trump. Served as FBI Director from 2001-2013.

SAP --- Special Access Program, a security protocol used by the U.S. federal government that provides highly classified information with safeguards and access restrictions that exceed those used for regular classified information.

Sauce --- Slang term derived from the word "source." When information is provided on 4chan, 8chan, or 8kun that is not common knowledge, the

GLOSSARY

one posting the information will frequently be asked to provide a source (sauce).

Snowden --- Edward Snowden, the former CIA employee and NSA contractor who stole and made public two classified NSA surveillance programs—PRISM and XKeyscore.

Snow White --- A signature by Q referring to the CIA, so named because of the Agency's seven supercomputers that are named after the seven dwarves.

The Bloody Wonderland --- Q's reference to Saudi Arabia, which was notorious in the past for its frequent use of public execution.

Unmask --- Exposing the concealed name of a U.S. person in surveillance data.

Vault 7 --- A series of documents published by WikiLeaks in 2017 that detail the capabilities of the CIA to perform electronic surveillance and cyber warfare.

Wet Works --- Slang for assassination. The term was used in the John Podesta emails published by WikiLeaks.

WH --- White House, the official residence and workplace of the President of the United States. White House is also used as a metonym for the President and his advisors.

Where we go one, we go all --- A line from the film White Squall which was based on the sinking of a school Brigantine sailing ship in 1961. The phrase "Where we go one, we go all" is a signature found in many of Q's posts.

Who performs in a circus? --- Clowns, which is a reference to the CIA; an agency also known as Clowns in America.

Wizards & Warlocks --- An internal name used by NSA employees and contractors—guardians of all electronic information.

WL --- WikiLeaks, a watchdog organization founded by Julian Assange that publishes documents leaked from various government and corporate sources.

GLOSSARY

WRWY --- We are with you.

WWG1WGA --- The abbreviation for "Where we go one, we go all," a line from the film White Squall which was based on the sinking of a school Brigantine sailing ship in 1961. The phrase "Where we go one, we go all" is a signature found in many of Q's posts.

Y --- Generally, refers to the goat head and owl symbolism, images, and icons used by the occult. It has also been used in references to former FBI Director James Come[Y] and with reference to his book, A Higher Loyalty [Y].

CONCLUSION

The use of information and misinformation as a strategic weapon to manipulate or weaken a population is not a new concept. Information and misinformation have always had a way of spreading like wildfire and sowing seeds and content throughout history.

However, the rapid growth of technology and communication and the ubiquity of information have greatly complicated how we interact with information. The military and government find themselves struggling to keep up with this rapid evolution of warfare. Meanwhile, the rest of the larger civilian population find that information warfare is not a concept that applies only to the battlefield. The information war is pervasive, but it is also imprecise and difficult to narrow down. Information warfare bleeds into our everyday life. From social media to the news, our online presence is opening ourselves up to potential exploitation by the information war.

This text aimed to educate more people about the state of the information war, but to also remind people that they do have some say in the matter. Again, it bears repeating that although the information war seems like something for Silicon Valley executives and military personnel, it is not beyond the regular civilian to take responsibility for their part in the information war. Remember, the flow of information has many vectors,

CONCLUSION

which means your interaction with it can define a number of other interactions with information.

As such, it is important to take the tactics we put forward in this text and incorporate them into your daily life. It does not matter where you are positioned in society or how small your opinion might be, who knows what impact you can make. The worst thing you could let yourself do is become passive to the information war. You could easily become a person who takes things at face value but challenge yourself to stand up and take action.

Misinformation, propaganda, and the like get passed around much easier when no one questions it. Make better use of your social media accounts and do your part in turning the tide of the information war. Those who perceive or understand it too late run the risk of simply being caught up in the whirlwind of change. Lastly, remember that you are a part of a larger community. Regardless of the difference in ideals and beliefs, we are relying on one another to build up our nation's information strategies and security.

At the end of the day, the direction of this information war is hard to determine. Moreover, its implications are even harder to fully grasp. Will the United States government and military overcome their current struggles and vulnerabilities to fully exploit and integrate the powers and advantages of information warfare? Or will the information revolution completely transform the face of warfare and change the way civilians engage with information? The uncertainties are endless. However, what does remain is the understanding that the information war is all-encompassing. The revolution began a long time ago and who knows how much longer it will carry on for.

We hope this text opened your eyes to the ever-changing world of information warfare, its concepts, and its implications. This is a revolution that began as a change in concepts, but became a revolution in technology, equipment, strategy and tactics. Perhaps, you have gained a better understanding of your place in society and how you can enact change. Moreover, we encourage you to take that understanding and turn it into action, no matter how small and minute. Be the mosquito in the quiet room of passive acceptance. Be the candle in the dark room of misinformation.

www.ingramcontent.com/pod-product-compliance
Lightning Source LLC
Chambersburg PA
CBHW071710020426
42333CB00017B/2207